MODERN

MODERN

JONATHAN GLANCEY

RIZZOLI
NEW YORK

MODERN

First published in the United States of
America in 1999 by
RIZZOLI INTERNATIONAL
PUBLICATIONS, INC.
300 Park Avenue South, New York, NY 10010

ISBN 0-8478-2211-7
LC 99-70297

Chief contributor **Graham Vickers**

Executive editor **Judith More**
Executive art editor **Janis Utton**
Project editor **Julia North**
Editor **Arlene Sobel**
Layout designer **Tony Spalding**
Production controllers **Rachel Staveley,
Paul Hammond**
Picture research **Nadine Bazar**
Indexer **Ann Parry**

Set in Neue Hevetica
Produced by Toppan Printing Company
Limited
Printed in Hong Kong

Right *Saarinen House by Charles Eames*

Title page *The Dome House by Bernard Judge*

CONTENTS

INTRODUCTION

Modern. We use the word so often that we rarely stop to think what it means. It derives from the Latin "modo", meaning "just now" or "right now". It has been a feature of the English language and Latin languages for a very long time, even though, when we are thinking about art, design, and architecture, we associate its use almost exclusively with the 20th century and possibly beyond. We find it hard to imagine that architects and designers

in previous centuries thought of themselves as Moderns, yet they did, and self-consciously so. During the first quarter of the 18th century, as the Palladian style of architecture developed in Britain before spreading to the United States, its champions and practitioners described themselves as Moderns. So did their critics. When we look at photographs of Palladian buildings like Lord Burlington's Chiswick House in west London, or Thomas Jefferson's University of Virginia at Charlottesville, or step inside their exquisitely proportioned interiors, we sense a connection between these Classical designs and the chaste, white architecture of the early Modern Movement which took root in Europe, mainly in France and Germany, some two centuries later.

What the Palladian buildings and those of the Modern Movement have in common is not simply restraint and chasteness, but a sense of mathematical purity and, above all, the sort of clean lines that rightly suggest that their designers were reacting against what must have been overelaborate styles of the past. And, indeed, they were. The Palladians were fierce polemicists who believed that the Baroque style that they were brought up with – in England in the long shadow of Christopher Wren, Nicholas Hawksmoor, and John Vanbrugh – was overwrought, bulbous, and vulgar. It had moved too far away from the purity of the ancient architects of Rome and the rules of architecture laid down by Vitruvius in the 1st century, which held that the orders of architecture – the essential trilogy of Doric, Ionic, and Corinthian – could answer every architectural requirement.

The self-styled Modern architects of the 20th century had much the same feeling about the European architecture of the late 19th and early 20th centuries. Not only was it believed to be excessive in a similar way that Palladians thought Baroque to be, but it was also decadent. More than this, the fussy, "wedding cake" or fantasy styles that led up to the First World War were seen

as irrelevant and belonging to a defunct era. Laced, lavished, and decked in a potpourri of *faux* historical treatments, these buildings were seen by Modernists as a denial of the reality of the new machine age. After the carnage of the Great War (1914–8), there was only one way to go for the architects and designers of the Modern Movement – and that was toward the future. In Le Corbusier's famous phrase, the house itself – the touchstone of architecture and to a large extent our humanity – would be a "machine for living in".

Left The Arts and Crafts designs of William Morris (1834–96), as seen in this wallpaper with its intricate foliage, harkened back to a rustic simplicity. The Arts and Crafts Movement challenged fussy 19th-century style and opened the way for the Modern Movement to flourish.

In both the early 18th and early 20th centuries, Modern was as much a creed – messianic, zealous – as it was a description of a desire by those who shaped our built world to walk away from the past. There was, of course, a difference between the two generations of Moderns. The earlier breed looked backward beyond the Baroque to the purity of the architecture of Inigo Jones of a century before (the Queen's House, Greenwich, and the Banqueting Hall, Whitehall, both in London, were the focus of the Palladians' admiration), and thence to Andrea Palladio in 16th-century Veneto, and beyond even this peerless architect to Vitruvius, and thus the Golden Age of Rome under the Emperor Augustus. In other words, although they were radicals in the true sense of reaching back to what they saw as the roots of civilized architecture and design, they were Classicists through and through.

Below Gamble House, in Pasadena, California, is America's most famous Arts and Crafts building. Designed by Charles and Henry Greene in 1908–9, it displays superb craftsmanship and a simple design that was to have a lasting effect on Modernism.

On the other hand, the 20th-century brood, to whom this book is dedicated, looked forward. They were radicals in the sense in which we tend to use the word today: they wanted to change the world, to spike the canons of 19th-century design and its historical style-mongering. In fact, for the earliest of the 20th-century Moderns, there would be no such thing as style in the future. Architecture and design were to be styleless – if in practice very often stylish – and were to be functional responses to the needs of the machine age. It was as if the Modern Movement were trying to establish a cultural Year Zero.

This was an all but impossible goal. History is ultimately inescapable. Even those undisputed masters of the Modern Movement, Mies van der Rohe (see pp.20–1) and Le Corbusier (see pp.18–9), were in love with the architecture of ancient Greece. These greats stood between two worlds, that of Classical

Right *In this desk lamp
by Joseph Hoffman (1901)
for Woka, all of the Classical
elements have been
stripped to a minimum.*

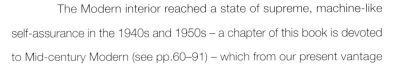

learning and that of the truly Modern world that they only just saw in the
world of the computer, mass communications, mass travel, space
exploration, new materials, technology, and what we call Globalism. And
yet, as the pages of this book show, architects and designers soon
began to react against the puritanical and overly rational endeavours of
the early Modern Movement as the truly Modern world described here
came into being. The more advanced science and technology became,
the more architects and designers were inclined to retreat into history as,
perhaps, we do to childhood comforts when we feel ill, or simply unable
to face up to the insistence of our Modern world.

The Modern interior reached a state of supreme, machine-like
self-assurance in the 1940s and 1950s – a chapter of this book is devoted
to Mid-century Modern (see pp.60–91) – which from our present vantage
point appear far more glamorous decades than they did to those who reacted so fiercely against this style
from the mid-1960s. Then they appeared to be too clinical – a step too far in the creation of a universal
architecture that, superficially, appeared to allow no concessions to either local sensibilities or the messy
vitality of everyday life. A retreat from the high days of Modernism was in the offing.

The retreat, though, was artful and knowing and often simply arch. Its manifestation in architecture
and design – Post-Modernism – was a concept well-known to philosophers, novelists, and literary critics
before it was applied to the built world. Post-Modernism, as you can see for yourself on pages 120 to 135,
plundered the book of historical styles in an intentionally ironic manner. It was as if designers could no longer
face up to the rigours of the Modern Movement as it had been established by the Bauhaus (see pp.16–7), by
Mies van der Rohe, and by Le Corbusier in the 1920s. Yet, starting in the mid-1980s, the generation

Right *All light and air:
Hill House (1902-3),
Helensburgh, Ayrshire,
Scotland, by Charles Rennie
Mackintosh, has a sense
and sensibility that was to
inform the Modern house.*

that followed the Post-Moderns
reacted against what it saw
as the frivolous and ultimately
decadent nature of Post-Modern
design. Just as the Palladians
had looked back to their
Classical roots some 250 years
earlier, so the New Moderns, to
group together a variety of
talents for the moment, looked
back to the purity of the early

Modern Movement. At the end of the 20th century, many of the best young architects and designers were working in a clean-cut idiom. No irony. No jokes. Yet they differ from the pioneers of the Modern Movement in that they moved in a number of very different, if albeit related, directions. At one extreme there was the Minimalist approach that was best exemplified by John Pawson (see pp.140–1); at the other extreme was the technological aesthetic of Richard Rogers (see pp.100–1) or of Future Systems (see pp.104–5). In between these there were approaches that ranged from a Modern form of Baroque (known as Neo-Baroque, see pp.106–19) to a sensitive and even sensual Modernism that is seen at its best in the interiors of the New York architect Lee Mindel (see pp.154–5).

Left The strong curves, abstract patterns, and biomorphic designs of the Belgian architect and designer, Henry van de Velde (1863–1957), are epitomized in this Art Nouveau setting that he designed.

Even then, it is important to bear in mind, that, apart from the mainstream of the Modern Movement, there were a number and variety of cross-currents and back-waters that also fit into the story of Modern architecture and design. The organic wonders of the Catalan architect Antoni Gaudí (see pp.34–5) were, for example, a new form of design. It was described as *Modernismo* in its day, although it has nothing to do with the rectilinear world of the Bauhaus and its disciples. Nor, really, did the excesses of Pop design (see pp.80–91), and certainly not the attempts by architects like Sir Edwin Lutyens (see pp.50–1) or decorators like David Hicks (see pp.58–9) to create new forms of Classical design.

The variety of the Modern experience is great, and yet, throughout, it is shot through with a sense of creating radically new worlds or radically new ways of looking at old ways of shaping the four walls that surround us. The aim of this book is to uncover and revel in the Modern styles of the 20th century as they have affected the design of the home.

Each of the homes shown here constitutes a powerful design statement. Each has been influential, some for the equivalent of Andy Warhol's "15 minutes of fame", others throughout the 20th century and into the 21st. Collectively, they represent the 20th century's perennial attempt to find new ways of representing the idea of house and home, and each, in its own way, is Modern.

Below The swooping yet functional forms of a Thonet bentwood rocking chair Model 7500 (c.1880) are proof that Modern design could be highly expressive, yet lightweight and free of gratuitous decoration.

THE MODERN MOVEMENT

The Modern Movement was nothing less than a revolution in taste, in style, in the whole philosophy of architecture and design. It was perhaps the first time that architects, artists, designers, novelists, playwrights, poets, musicians, and philosophers rebelled against history. At its most extreme the decorations and canons of taste that had evolved over many centuries and even millennia were to be abandoned. A new aesthetic was needed, one that the most zealous Modernists believed

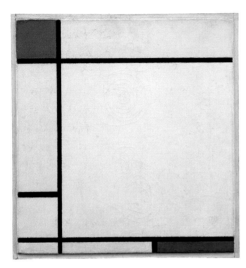

Above *Piet Mondrian's study of grids influenced the architecture of the early Modern Movement. The painting's three-dimensional counterpart can be found in the work of De Stijl architects, notably Gerrit Rietveld.*

Below right *This illustration from Le Corbusier's* Vers une Architecture *(1923) shows an ideal home for blue-collar workers – with air, sunlight, space, and a place to exercise.*

Previous page (left) *The living room in the Maison de Verre (1932) in Paris, by Pierre Chareau and Bernard Bijvoet, uses mass-produced, flexibly planned components.*

Previous page (right) *This furniture catalogue for Wohnbedarf was designed by Herbert Mayer, a teacher at the Bauhaus, in 1934.*

to represent a new epoch, the age of the machine. In reality, the Modern Movement was a complex phenomenon and it would be unwise to attempt to package it too neatly. Even so, there are clear markers in its history, key players in its development, and a number of buildings and interiors that define and characterize this cultural revolution.

The roots of the Modern Movement lay in the reaction of artists of all kinds to the rise of the machine age. It was clear that the Industrial Revolution had changed human life profoundly, and yet the response of architects and their clients was, for the most part, to try to deny the emergence of a new culture, or cloak it in such a way that would make it more acceptable to a part-fearful and part-fascinated public. For example, when the first passenger railway locomotives emerged in the 1830s, their engineers employed the Classical vocabulary of ornament as a decorative device: thus chimneys were cast in the guise of Corinthian columns, and splashers and domes were gartered with Grecian friezes and Roman garlands. But, as engineers became more confident and ever busier as the 19th century steamed on, such decoration was not so much abandoned as forgotten. The same applied to architecture, where a distinction was made by architects and critics between "honest" as opposed to "dishonest" buildings. The former were designed as a true response to the needs of the machine age, while the latter continued, in ever more desperate and unlikely ways, to be couched in *faux* forms or revived historical guises.

Engineers became the heroes of the new aesthetic, and therefore it comes as no surprise that Le Corbusier's hugely influential book, *Vers une Architecture (Toward a New Architecture)* (1923), was copiously illustrated with images of cars, locomotives, ships, airplanes, bridges, and grain silos. The purity of their design, freed from the perceived tyranny of historical style-mongering, was paraded as a virtue that architects needed to adopt. And soon. It does seem remarkable, with the benefit of hindsight, to find the gardener Joseph Paxton designing the Crystal Palace in London (1851) – a beacon of Modern sensibility – at least 50 years before architects were to achieve such purity of form, such a perfect marriage between form and function.

But the rejection of stifling historical styles was one thing; the development of a new aesthetic

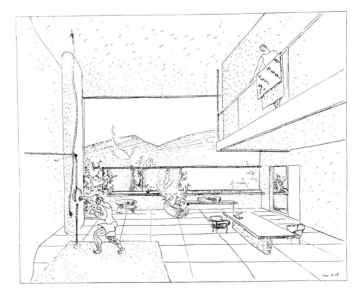

that was redolent of the machine age was another. And yet what should this new architecture look like? The styles of the past had developed incrementally, but in this case the need for a new style was instant. (Interestingly, the dilemma was to find echoes in the ultra-rapid digital revolution in the second half of the 20th century – what should a computer-driven culture look like?)

In the early 1900s *avant-garde* thinking provided the key, at first emanating from Paris in the form of Cubism, and then from a legendary German state school in which industrial design, fine arts, architecture, and crafts were treated as a single enmeshed discipline: the Bauhaus (see pp.16–7). In Paris, between 1905 and 1910, Pablo Picasso and Georges Braques explored a new form of expression – on canvas – that within 15 to 20 years was to find an echo in the early work of Le Corbusier (see pp.18–9). Equally, the geometric experiments of the Dutch artist Piet Mondrian signalled the emergence of a new and purist aesthetic that, applied to architecture and design, was to help change the look and experience of our homes, our architecture, and our cities.

This is not to say that architects were waiting hopelessly in the wings. In Germany, a group of architects and designers formed the Deutscher Werkbund in 1907, which led to the founding of the Bauhaus by Walter Gropius (1883–1969) in 1919. The Bauhaus experiment was crucial to the development of Modern architecture and design, fusing the experiments of artists, craft-workers, and architects. By the outbreak of the First World War, Gropius had already begun to point out the direction that Modern architecture was to take. The Bauhaus had provided an invaluable focus, pulling together strands of ideology, aesthetics, and socio-economics inside stylized headquarters whose influential image was greatly to outstrip its brief physical existence. Having brought together diverse disciplines, the Bauhaus would, after the First World War, endure as a powerful symbol of art and industry harnessed together to serve idealized social objectives. Ironically, its greatest impact was in America, where émigré Gropius became Professor of Architecture at Harvard.

And so, when the post-First World War map of Europe was re-drawn, a Modern architecture and design aesthetic truly began to emerge. Its principles would endure, variously interpreted, throughout the remainder of the century.

Left *A true "machine 'a habiter": this early 1930s American interior was designed by Donald Deskey and Edward Durrell Stone. The polished aluminium staircase was designed by Deskey and was inspired by the new technology. Glass bricks were new at the time.*

Below *The cantilevered B32 chromed-steel chair is by Marcel Breuer (1928). The structure was inspired by Breuer's rethinking of the bars on bicycles.*

Left Walter Gropius's house in Lincoln, Massachusetts, is a mixture of steely Modern Movement furniture – largely by Marcel Breuer – and luxurious materials. The rooms are bathed in the maximum amount of daylight.

Right The Breuer House in New Canaan, Connecticut, features wooden furniture inspired by the Bauhaus ethos of "form follows function".

BAUHAUS

PROFILE

DURATION:
1919–33

EDUCATORS:
Walter Gropius, 1883–1969
Paul Klee, 1879–1940
Oskar Schlemmer, 1888–1943
Vassily Kandinsky, 1886–1944
Johannes Itten, 1888–1967
Josef Albers, 1886–1976
László Maholy-Nagy, 1895–1946
Hannes Meyer, 1889–1954
Marcel Breuer, 1902–81
Ludwig Mies van der Rohe, 1886–1969

PRINCIPAL PROJECTS:
Bauhaus Building, Dessau, Germany, by Walter Gropius, 1925

The Bauhaus (construction house) was the most influential school and research institute of the early Modern Movement. It was created in Weimar in 1919, as was the new, post-war German republic, and it rose and fell with it – destroyed by the Nazi government. Bauhaus was a successor of the Deutscher Werkbund, which in turn had its roots – and shared concerns – in the Arts and Crafts Movement, most particularly, what was the best way of connecting machine-age production to art.

The Bauhaus was far more than the sum of its parts: its radical zeal and dynamism was to resound throughout Europe and America. Many of the school's most gifted teachers settled in America after Hitler seized power in 1933. This was not simply because many were Jews; rather, none was able to practise the new form of art and design they had developed in Weimar and at Dessau under Hitler, whose preference was for Neo-classicism for public monuments and a "gingerbread" style for housing. Mies van der Rohe (see pp.20–1), appointed director after Gropius left first for Britain and then America, tried to keep the Bauhaus flag flying, but he made no headway. In 1937 he, too, left for America and a hugely successful career as one of the century's greatest architects. The Bauhaus brought all the creative arts together under the steely gaze of the Modernist eye; as Gropius put it, "the Bauhaus strives to collect all artistic creativity into a unity, to reunite all artistic disciplines into a new architecture". And it did.

Left *A double-height living room in an apartment in Unité d'Habitation, the magnificent 17-storey building that has been imitated but never bettered. It makes unapologetic use of raw concrete, and maximum use of sunlight and shadow.*

Right *"Architecture," said Le Corbusier, "is the masterly, correct and magnificent play of masses brought together in light", as seen in a living room in Le Roche-Jeanneret House.*

LE CORBUSIER

PROFILE

BORN:

La Chaux-de-Fonds, Switzerland, 1887 (d.1966)

EDUCATED:

Trained as a metal engraver; self-taught as an architect; worked with Peter Behrens in Berlin and Auguste Perret in Paris

PRINCIPAL COMMISSIONS:

Le Roche-Jeanneret House, Paris, 1923

Pavilion de L'Esprit Nouveau, Paris, 1925

Villa Savoye, Poissy-sur-Seine, France, 1931

Unité d'Habitation, Marseille, France, 1947–52

Pilgrimage Chapel of Notre Dame-du-haut, Ronchamp, France, 1955

The greatest, most inventive, and most influential architect of the 20th century, Le Corbusier (the professional name of Charles-Edouard Jeanneret) was a craftsman, journalist, polemicist, painter, sculptor, radical thinker, and architect. A loner, he was a deeply religious man, acutely aware of his Waldensian background: he was descended from the few Cathars who had survived the Inquisition, and whose doctrines undermined the foundations of the Roman Catholic Church. His history imbued him with a mission to reconnect with his past, and to fight against social, religious, and artistic orthodoxy throughout his hugely creative life. The Picasso of architecture, his style changed over the years (often puzzling and upsetting his less adventurous followers), from the crisp, white Cubism of his early Paris period (Le Roche-Jeanneret House, a "machine for living in"), to the brooding, sculptural, raw concrete period after the Second World War, and finally into steel and the seemingly High-Tech (Zurich Pavilion, 1967, completed after his death).

Le Corbusier also designed superb furniture (with Charlotte Perriand), still in production today. In addition, he wrote the most important Modern Movement polemic, *Vers une Architecture* (*Toward a New Architecture*), in 1923; devised a proportional system of his own ("*Le Modulor*"); and, heroically, was never sucked into the architectural establishment.

Left Farnsworth House is
the stuff of Modern dreams –
a leather daybed (1930),
"Barcelona" chair (1929),
a blazing fire, superb wood
partitions, daylight, and views.

Right The Mies fireplace
in the Farnsworth House
shows the layered hierarchy
of materials – stone,
stainless steel, and wood.

MIES VAN DER ROHE

PROFILE

BORN:

Aachen, Germany, 1886
(d.1969)

EDUCATED:

Worked with Bruno Paul and
Peter Behrens in Berlin

PRINCIPAL COMMISSIONS:

Weissenhof Housing, Stuttgart,
  Germany, 1926
Hermann Lange House,
  Krefeld, Germany, 1928
German Pavilion, Barcelona,
  Spain, 1929
Tugendhat House, Brno,
  Czech Republic, 1930
Farnsworth House, Plano,
  Illinois,1951
Lake Shore Drive Apartments,
  Chicago, Illinois, 1951
Crown Hall, Chicago, Illinois,
  1956
Seagram Building (with Philip
  Johnson), New York, 1958
Neue Nationalgaleri, Berlin,
  1968

The son of a stonemason, Mies van der Rohe trained in his father's building yard. Later he was apprenticed to the German architect Peter Behrens (1886–1940), a pioneering corporate designer dedicated to shaping every physical expression of a client's organization. These influences of craftsmanship and holistic design are evident in Mies's own work, the ultimate goal of which was to create a Modern architecture incorporating the purity of Neo-classical buildings. At first Mies emulated the Neo-classical work of Friedrich Schinkel (1781–1841) until finding his own voice as a truly Modern architect in the early 1920s.

Mies's now-famous design for the German Pavilion at Barcelona's 1929 National Exhibition took the form of a minimalist arrangement of vertical travertine slabs and glass panels beneath a reinforced concrete roof-slab supported on columns of chrome-plated steel. A manipulation of space by the simplest of planes, it was reworked soon afterwards in Mies's Tugendhat House in Brno, in the Czech Republic, built for Dr Edith Farnsworth. The exhibition had featured his "Barcelona" chair (still a modern corporate icon) and the house would include an expanded range of his elegantly spare furniture. After a brief tenure as director of the Bauhaus (see pp.16–7) in 1930, Mies emigrated to America where his most famous structure remains the rigorously Modernist Seagram Building on Manhattan's Park Avenue. This monolithic skyscraper was in itself enough to ensure that Mies would become a totemic figure, signifying a Modern design aesthetic founded upon reduction and simplicity.

Left *The stairs of the Villa Mairea are based partly on a traditional Japanese bamboo screen and partly on the idea of a walk through a Scandinavian forest.*

Right *This highly sculpted corner fireplace in the Villa Mairea is a Modern interpretation of the traditional Scandinavian hearth.*

ALVAR AALTO

PROFILE

BORN:

Kuortane, Finland, 1898
(d.1976)

EDUCATED:

Helsinki Polytechnic, Helsinki

PRINCIPAL COMMISSIONS:

Prefabricated Apartment
  House, Turku, Finland, 1927–8
Artek furniture (from 1928)
Convalescent Home, Paimio,
  Finland, 1929–33
Municipal Library, Viipuri,
  Finland, 1930–5
Architect's own house,
  Helsinki, 1934–6
Villa Mairea, Noormakku,
  Finland, 1935–9
Baker House Hall of Residence,
  Massachusetts Institute of
  Technology, Cambridge,
  Massachusetts, 1947–9
Cultural Centre, Helsinki,
  1955–8

Aalto is widely respected for having brought a warm, natural, and human touch to the severity of the high Modern Movement. Unlike so many Modern Movement designers, his buildings have a way of, if not blending into the Finnish landscape, then working in harmony with it. Brought up in a land of lakes, forests, and glorious light, his many buildings – private and public – are often exquisite essays or tone poems in the use of light and landscape. It was not simply in his use of materials, although he made considerable and original use of timber, but in the ways that he softened the focus of Modern architecture, that encourages us to see him as an architect whose work is as much "organic" (or close to nature) as it is rigorous and functional.

Aalto began designing furniture and fittings for his own buildings at an early stage in his career in collaboration with his wife Aino Marsio, a fellow architect whom he married in 1925. The pieces they produced have become icons of Modern design, and have continued in production. As a result, Aalto interiors, like those of Frank Lloyd Wright (see pp.36–7) or Antoni Gaudí (see pp.34–5), are very much of a piece, from fabrics and rugs to chairs, tables, trolleys, and door handles. And yet, because of the gentle nature of Aalto's designs, the overall effect is never overbearing. Aalto's was a Modernism with a human face. As with so many of those architects who fought at the front in the First World War, Aalto sought to create a new architecture that offered fresh air, sunlight, and a sense of complete and natural freedom.

Left The studio sitting room of Schindler's own home is of exposed wood, canvas, and glass construction, with a concrete floor. The furniture is by Schindler.

Right Daylight is brought into the Schindler House through narrow, vertical slits, as well as clerestories and other devices, resulting in a subtle and ever-shifting play of light throughout.

RUDOLPH SCHINDLER

PROFILE

BORN:

Vienna, 1887 (d.1953)

EDUCATED:

Technische Hochschule, Vienna

PRINCIPAL COMMISSIONS:

Schindler House, Los Angeles, California, 1923

Lovell Beach House, Newport, California, 1926

Buck Residence, Los Angeles, California, 1934

Walker House, Los Angeles, California, 1935–6

Falk House, Los Angeles, California, 1939–40

Tischer House, Westwood, Los Angeles, California, 1949–50

Rudolf Schindler came to Los Angeles just before the outbreak of the First World War. He saw California as a kind of "new found land" in which, freed from the stifling bourgeois strictures of his native Vienna (despite the revelations by fellow Viennese radicals – Freud in psychology, Wittgenstein in philosophy, and Loos in architecture), he could set about a new and liberated architecture.

The house he built for himself, his family, and bohemian entourage in Los Angeles, is a near-timeless Modern masterpiece. It enjoyed a resurgence of interest in the late 1990s as it seemed to promise a Modernism that was disciplined and thoughtful, and yet somehow natural and romantic. Screened by a sea of waving bamboo, the single-storey house is made of wood and comprises four studios, a guest wing, and a garage. The doors, inspired by traditional Japanese houses, are sliding screens. These open the house into the interlocking gardens in ways that make it difficult to tell where the interior ends and the world outside begins. Importantly, Schindler demonstrated that a house could be made of simple, lightweight materials and enjoy the feel of a year-round holiday home. This was truly a liberation from the heavy-duty and encrusted architecture of pre-war Vienna. The furniture is at one with the house, as is every strikingly simple detail in the kitchens and bathrooms. Perhaps Schindler's most striking building, however, is another private dwelling, the Lovell Beach House at Newport Beach, California, a spatially sophisticated transatlantic echo of De Stijl by the ocean.

Left *The Maslan Residence in Cathedral City, California, demonstrates the open, flowing space sought and achieved by the best Modern designers. The walls – little more than partitions – are almost as delicate as the paper screens in traditional Japanese houses.*

Right *The living room of the Maslan Residence has a circular opening for sunlight, and mirrors to increase the depth of the horizontal space. The chairs and coffee table are by Mies van der Rohe.*

RICHARD NEUTRA

PROFILE

BORN:

Vienna, 1892 (d.1970)

EDUCATED:

Technische Hochschule, Vienna

PRINCIPAL COMMISSIONS:

Lovell House, Los Angeles, California, 1927–9

Josef von Sternberg House, Los Angeles, California, 1936

Channel Heights Housing Project, San Pedro, California, 1942–4

Kaufmann House, Palm Springs, California, 1946–7

Tremaine House, Santa Barbara, California, 1947–8

Maslan Residence, Cathedral City, California, 1962

Along with Rudolph Schindler (see pp.24–5), Neutra created the style of domestic architecture that says California as surely as a song by the Beach Boys. The style is apparently effortless – transparent houses that open out to the elements and welcome nature into the heart of Modernism. The architecture is always crisp, and yet the spirit of the setting is entirely relaxed. Neutra brought the intellectual weight and artistic certainty of Vienna, where he trained with Adolf Loos (see pp.52–3), and Berlin, where he worked with Erich Mendelsohn, to the sunny west coast of the United States.

Neutra had emigrated to Chicago in 1923, and began working with Frank Lloyd Wright (see pp.36–7), before moving to Los Angeles, where he temporarily teamed up with his fellow Austrian, Schindler. Neutra's search was for a form of domestic architecture that could be "a harbour for the soul", unadorned in itself, yet adorned by the landscape it stood in. He said he wanted to create "a slice of eternity", and in the design of the Kaufmann desert house in Palm Springs he came close to it. In later years Neutra teamed up with Robert E. Alexander (until 1958), and then with his own son, Dion, but his star faded almost as quickly as it had risen. He was never to repeat the success of the stunning houses that he built in the 1930s and 1940s.

EILEEN GRAY

PROFILE

BORN:

Dublin, Ireland, 1878 (d.1976)

EDUCATED:

Slade School of Art, London;
self-taught as an architect
and designer

PRINCIPAL COMMISSIONS:

Ceramics (private commissions),
furniture, and lacquerware
(many are still in production)
E.1027 House, Roquebrune,
France, 1927–9
Apartment for Susan Talbot,
Paris, 1933

Eileen Gray built very little, but what little she did has long captured the imagination of those for whom Modernism and sensuality can be exciting partners. Gray's contribution to the Modern house was to demonstrate that it could be at once ascetic and luxurious – to her, not a contradiction in terms.

A wealthy woman brought up in a stifling and old-fashioned environment, Gray broke from her family, settled in France, and led a productive yet bohemian existence in Paris and the south coast. Here she built her own villa, which was admired by, among others, Le Corbusier (see pp.18–9), who had built a seaside cabin nearby. The interior made extensive use of her beautifully wrought furniture, lamps, rugs, and mirrors, several of which have become 20th-century classics. Gray was a free spirit, who never aligned herself with an artistic or architectural movement. Her designs were expensive and lavish, and so could only be had by herself or wealthy patrons. Her use of sliding screens and illuminated glass floors brought a sense of the fantastic and filmic into Modern design.

Eileen Gray designed her
client Susan Talbot's bedroom
in her apartment in Paris with
the quality of a Hollywood
film set. The floor is made
of translucent glass panels
illuminated from below.
Animal skins complement
the voluptuous forms of
Gray's "Bibendum" chairs
(1925–6) and exquisite
decorative pieces.

ORGANIC

"The straight line belongs to Man," said Antoni Gaudí, "the curve to God." Most of us know what the architect of the biomorphic Expiatory Temple of the Holy Family (the Sagrada Família) in Barcelona meant. For Gaudí the straight line was a problem because it spoke of the tyranny of the mathematical or clockwork model of the universe that modern man had created for himself. The truth, of course, is that Gaudí was a great, if intuitive, mathematician. The geometric complexity of the Sagrada Família has

been a mind-stretching problem for those completing this great temple at the end of the century. Nevertheless, Gaudí's buildings are close to nature because they borrow from the richness of forms of geometry and structure found in the natural world. His superb apartment buildings in Barcelona really do look and feel like giant plants or as-yet unclassified living, breathing animals. In this sense they are Organic.

However, the word Organic has meant many things to different people. Louis Sullivan, the great Chicago architect who taught Frank Lloyd Wright (see pp.36–7), described himself as an Organic architect even though his buildings have little of Gaudí's animal or vegetable characteristics. Sullivan's Organic aesthetic was reserved for the decoration that adorned his solid, mineral-like buildings. Wright also used the word to describe his architecture. By Organic he meant that every part of a house – from window latches and door hinges, to roofs and chimneys, to chairs and cupboards – should be all of a piece. This is certainly true of the very many houses Wright built. In fact, Wright insisted that he had at all times complete control of the design of every last detail of the houses he designed; he was infamous for striding theatrically into clients' homes and smashing vases and other decorative gewgaws he disapproved of from the tables and mantelshelves with a sweep of his cane.

Significantly, in another time and another place – Communist Hungary in the 1970s – the rebel architect Imre Makovecz (see pp.42–3), a fan of Wright, developed, in theory and in practice, his notion of the "building being". For Makovecz, the natural or Organic house should follow the fundamental asymmetry of the human body: the house as a living, breathing, protective body that we inhabit, rather than Le Corbusier's finely tuned machine (see pp.18–9). Like Gaudí, Makovecz designed his buildings with more or less fully expressed animal and vegetable characteristics – frog-like eyes and lizard-like skins.

This organic style had, and has, its special logic and should not be confused with hippie notions of Organic lifestyles. Nevertheless, American architects Bruce Goff (see pp.40–1) and Herb Greene pursued a fundamentally escapist form of architecture in the 1950s and 1960s, premised on alternative lifestyles well away from the conceits, stresses, and constraints of city life. The Greene House in Norman, Oklahoma (1961), in particular, was a striking celebration of a pioneering way of life that has never really disappeared in the

United States between the Rockies and the Appalachians. However, the vast majority of people who choose an alternative lifestyle live in machine-built trailers rather than a lovingly crafted buffalo of a house like Greene's.

What, then, can we identify as Organic's unifying strand as a Modern design style, rather than as a back-to-nature philosophy and lifestyle? Essentially it is the broad story of the coming of age of manufactured materials and our attitudes toward them. The early decorative use of stylized leaves, flowers, and other natural motifs to "alleviate" the lines of *parvenu* industrial structures and products was symptomatic of a general unease about new technology.

Walter Crane, informal spokesman for the Arts and Crafts Movement, decried the whiplash lines of Art Nouveau as being the last gasp of a 19th-century obsession with decoration and the symptom of "a strange, decadent disease". The Organic preoccupations of Frank Lloyd Wright and his followers took the emphasis away from lines and placed it upon materials and the sympathetic juxtaposition of the man-made and the natural. Norman Foster's Willis Faber Building in Ipswich, England (1975), is in formal terms the very antithesis of an Organic design, and yet its high-insulation turf roof might fairly be seen as a Modern gesture toward linking a high-tech building to the Organic earth upon which it stands. Meanwhile, Javier Senosian Aguilar's elaborately dressed tunnellings beneath Mexico City (see pp.30, 32) represent a wish to get back to nature in the most literal sense – with a stylized hippie burrow for sophisticates.

The common link is the assumption that curved, naturally inspired shapes (often inferior in strict terms of mechanical efficiency) are somehow benignly symbolic of human qualities. They are a visual political assertion that we do not always have to choose the most rigorously efficient solution, and may elect instead to build into our dwellings and artefacts quotations from the lineaments of nature, usually translated into an artificial medium. The fact that Starck's monopod bar stools (right) are visually distanced from the Organic excrescences of Gaudí is evidence that we have acquired a more austere eye for the same sort of thing. As we have become increasingly comfortable with industrial products and materials, we are correspondingly more relaxed about "naturalizing" their shapes to make them seem more friendly. Organic, it could be argued, is therefore in the process of changing from being a "style" into becoming a legitimate part of the Modern vernacular.

Left Bones and organs were the inspiration for the style and construction of this carved oak armchair by Antoni Gaudí for Casa Calvet (1898–1900).

Below The bar stools at the Royalton Hotel in New York, by Philippe Starck, bear a striking resemblance to the legs of a deer.

Left *Curves abound in the walls and ceiling of a salon in the Casa Milá. The apartments are highly prized for their sinuous design, excellent planning, and glorious light.*

Right *At the entrance to the Casa Milá, serpentine "bone-like" wooden gates give way to frescoed walls and stone columns. Gaudí also used wooden "bone-like" imagery in his furniture designs.*

ANTONI GAUDI

PROFILE

BORN:
Reus, Spain, 1852 (d.1926)

EDUCATED:
Escuela Provincial de
Arquitectura, Barcelona,
Spain

PRINCIPAL COMMISSIONS:
Expiatory Temple of the Holy
  Family (Sagrada Família),
  Barcelona, 1883
Santa Coloma de Cervelló,
  Barcelona, 1898–1915
Palacio Güell, Barcelona,
  1886–9
Casa Batlló, Barcelona, 1904–6
Casa Milá (La Pedrera),
  Barcelona, 1906–10
Parque Güell, Barcelona,
  1900–14

The Spanish architect Antoni Gaudí achieved international fame for his synthesis of organic elements, traditional Catalan imagery, and imaginative technical solutions. His adopted city of Barcelona – at that time undergoing a cultural and political renaissance – was the centre of his activities. There he parlayed his version of Art Nouveau into a unique and highly dramatic aesthetic, exemplified by his Casa Batlló and Casa Milá apartment houses, and his elaborately self-indulgent (and still uncompleted) Sagrada Família church.

Gaudí lived the life of a religious ascetic, an uncompromising visionary whose working life coincided with a place and time that largely welcomed his vision and allowed him to create several buildings that proved highly influential. Gaudí's Organic, sinuous lines are intrinsic to his structures – they are not applied decoration but integrated elements, an expression of his favourite aphorism, "The straight line belongs to Man, the curve to God." The apartments in both Casa Batlló and Casa Milá conform to Gaudí's curvilinear aesthetic, challenging traditional design notions about domestic residences and – as early as 1904 – providing 20th-century designers with a seductive yet architecturally sound model for defining internal spaces by Organic shapes and imagery.

Left The strongly horizontal emphasis of Fallingwater is clear and the building's guiding geometric order is offset by natural finishes – like the rugged stone floor. Magnificent greenery is seen from the band of windows.

Right This corner detail shows the exterior wall blending with the room, and the subtle tracery of the windows.

FRANK LLOYD WRIGHT

PROFILE

BORN:
Chicago, Illinois, 1869
(d.1959)

EDUCATED:
Trained as an engineer at the University of Wisconsin, Wisconsin; trained as an architect in the office of Louis Sullivan

PRINCIPAL COMMISSIONS:
Robie House, Chicago, Illinois, 1908
Storer House, Los Angeles, California, 1912
Fallingwater, Bear Run, Pennsylvania, 1937–9
Johnson Wax Building, Racine, Wisconsin, 1936–9
Solomon R. Guggenheim Museum, New York, 1942–60

A native of Chicago, Frank Lloyd Wright drew inspiration from the midwestern prairies. In Fallingwater, a house set in the woods of Pennsylvania, Wright created a marriage between the outcrop of rock upon which the building sits (and which penetrates its living room) and a waterfall set in a vibrant surrounding landscape. Fallingwater is a complex arrangement of native stone verticals and poured-concrete cantilevered trays. This combination of man-made and natural materials reflected one of Wright's most fundamental tenets: harmony between structure and location. The same approach was carried through in every detail of the interior, affirming that for one of America's most prolific architects there was no distinction to be made between internal and external design: it was all of a piece.

From his early Chicago Prairie houses of the 1890s to the shell-like spiral of Manhattan's Guggenheim Museum (completed 1960 from a 1942 design), Wright explored a wide range of building designs, including family homes, skyscrapers, churches, government offices, bridges, and filling stations. In all he asserted the need to relate structure and materials to the architectural site. Fallingwater, completed when he was 70, is both typical in that it expresses his Organic concerns so lucidly, and atypical in that it strongly echoes Europe's International Modern (see pp.12–5) style, making its mark in America. Wright's legacy can be found in countless American homes where low, open-plan rooms spread into one another and terraces blend into the surrounding gardens.

Left *All of a piece: the Organically shaped dining room of Eliel Saarinen's home in Bloomfield Hills, Michigan, is echoed in the furniture, lighting, and the sculptural niches.*

Right *This detail of the dining room in the Saarinen Residence shows the rounded-back wooden chairs that were designed by the architect, which are consistent with the shape of the room.*

ELIEL SAARINEN

PROFILE

BORN:
Rantasalmi, Finland, 1873
(d.1950)

EDUCATED:
Helsinki University, Helsinki,
studying painting and
architecture

PRINCIPAL COMMISSIONS:
Hvitträsk, architect's own
    home, near Helsinki, 1901–2
Remer House, Brandenberg,
    Germany, 1905–8
Helsinki Railway Station,
    Helsinki, 1904–19
Cranbrook Academy of Art,
    Bloomfield Hills, Michigan,
    1926–43
General Motors Technical
    Center, Warren, Michigan
    (with Eero Saarinen),
    1948–56

Few architects live to work, as Eliel Saarinen did, in styles as widely divergent as the National Romanticism he practised with such conviction in Finland at the turn of the century, and the Mid-century Modernism he mastered in the United States with his son Eero half a century later. It was not that Saarinen was a natural eclectic, but he was an architect who understood the mood of the culture he was working in and was able to reflect that in buildings of great distinction.

The turning point came soon after the First World War, when commissions in Finland were very rare. Saarinen entered the competition to design the new *Chicago Tribune* headquarters. He came second, but the $20,000 prize money encouraged him, at 49, to emigrate to the States. His first great architectural achievement was the buildings for the Cranbrook School of Art, which became influential as a training school for American designers; in true Organic style, he designed everything down to the last door hinge. Later he worked on the seminal General Motors Technical Center, in Warren, Michigan. Its style was influenced by his son, Eero, who created the soaring, bird-like TWA Terminal at JFK airport near New York City. In the intervening years, Saarinen produced a range of Organic-style buildings. His work retained much of its Organic, Scandinavian roots even when, superficially, they appeared more Art Deco than Arts and Crafts.

Left *Bruce Goff's inventive approach to form and space often resulted in open-plan houses in the round, with the flow of space being continuous – as seen in the Samuel Ford House in Illinois.*

Right *The organic nature of his work can clearly be seen in this room in the Bavinger house in Oklahoma, dominated by rocks, water, and foliage.*

BRUCE GOFF

PROFILE

BORN:
Alton, Kansas, 1904 (d.1982)

EDUCATED:
Trained with Frank Lloyd Wright

PRINCIPAL COMMISSIONS:
Samuel Ford House, Aurora, Illinois, 1949
Bavinger House, Norman, Oklahoma, 1950–5
Gryder House, Ocean Springs, Missouri, 1960
Dace House, Beaver, Oklahoma, 1964
Glen Harder House, Mountain Lake, Missouri, 1970

Goff's houses look like escapees from Tolkien's *Lord of the Rings*. He created what he liked to call "gay spaces" – open-plan homes in the round that were very different in form and spirit from the four walls that surround conventional families. The result, after a large dose of Frank Lloyd Wright (see pp.36–7), was a small number of distinctive houses that focused on shared space – ideal places to meet and party, by the look and feel of them. By exploring alternative forms of domestic accommodation and ways of life, he was able to reconfigure the notion of the home into something more relaxed and less dogmatic. In his houses, the flow of space was continuous, and achieved by circular plans. He liked to compare his designs with the music of Debussy, and also with the writings of Gertrude Stein – her continuous beginnings reflected in the absence of orthogonal geometry.

Goff's principal creations were the Samuel Ford House in Illinois and the Bavinger House in Oklahoma. The former house was all but enclosed by a 50-metre (166-foot) diameter dome that was made of steel and sheathed in shingles. A central lantern topped by a glass spire brought daylight down into the impressive galleried interior. The latter house was comprised of a logarithmic spiral of social space that was contained by a continuous wall of unworked sandstone, with living rooms, stairs, access balconies, and the science-fiction roof suspended from a central mast by steel cables.

Left The Civic Hall in Visegrad, Hungary, contains the essential elements of a Makovecz house or shelter: a high timber roof held up by natural tree trunks and made by local carpenters, an old stove, and simple furniture.

Right The interior of the Civic Hall is constructed as though it were a forest: the roof and walls have been placed over and around a grove of tree trunks, which are both structural and decorative.

IMRE MAKOVECZ

PROFILE

BORN:

Budapest, Hungary, 1935

EDUCATED:

University of Budapest, Budapest, Hungary

PRINCIPAL COMMISSIONS:

Forestry buildings in and around Sventendre, Hungary, 1974–5

Catholic Church, Paks, Hungary, 1987–9

Hungarian Pavilion, Expo '92, Seville, Spain, 1992

Naturata Restaurant, Uberlinger, Germany, 1992

Makovecz became an architect by default: a rebel from his earliest days, when he blew up invading German tanks, and, later, opposed the Communist regime in Hungary, he was banned from conventional jobs and teaching posts. He worked first for a forestry department, where he began creating extraordinary zoomorphic buildings ("building beings" he calls them) for Hungarian forest campsites. Travelling with a band of carpenters and local builders, he constructed village halls in western Hungary, and then churches. The former took the form of giant wooden barns held up by tree trunks in place of stone columns or steel piers. The latter are womb-like structures crowned with domes and topped with tall, thin spires. There is a fairy-tale quality about his houses, too.

Makovecz is an intensely religious man, who is much influenced by Frank Lloyd Wright (see p.36–7) and the idea of the natural structure; his architecture both cossets and raises the spirit above the mundane. Makovecz also designs furniture and fittings, and has created buildings as diverse as a Catholic Church, in Paks, Hungary, and the Hungarian Pavilion at Expo '92 in Seville, Spain.

Left In the courtyard of the Truss Wall House, space flows out from the living room and around and up onto the roof. The house is finished inside and out in a white-painted, shell-like mortar; the furniture is mostly built into the walls.

Right The canvas-swathed walls of the Soft and Hairy House bedroom open onto a bathroom pod that is partly inside and partly outside in the central courtyard.

USHIDA FINDLAY

PROFILES

EISAKU USHIDA
BORN:
Tokyo, Japan, 1954

EDUCATED:
University of Tokyo, Japan

KATHRYN FINDLAY
BORN:
Glasgow, Scotland, 1950

EDUCATED:
Architectural Association, London

PRINCIPAL COMMISSIONS:
Echo Chamber House, Suginami, Tokyo, Japan, 1988–9
Truss Wall House, Tsurukawa, Tokyo, Japan, 1990–1
Chiaroscuro House, Tokyo, Japan, 1992–3
Soft and Hairy House, Ibaraki, Japan, 1992–3
Polyphony House, Osaka, Japan, 1995–7

Ushida Findlay represent a new mood in contemporary housing – a desire to create homes that are sensual and relaxed, where the world of private fantasies form the basis of a home, and the distinction between the structure and the natural landscape are blurred. They met in Tokyo in 1980: Findlay was studying at the Architectural Association in London; Ushida was working for Arata Isozaki (see pp.134–5) in Tokyo. Having set up in practice together, the architects now design houses that represent the dreams and desires of those who feel like outsiders, or for whom conventional homes are too restricting.

The forms they have created are Organic – amoeba-like as in the Truss Wall House; the stuff of a Dali sculpture in the delightfully named Soft and Hairy House. The geometries of these houses – each is different – are complex, echoing Gaudí (see pp.34–5), while the building methods can be unusual. The raised tiles of Truss Wall's courtyard were created by filling balloons with mortar, setting them in hexagonal moulds, and then opening them. Such houses are possible in the Tokyo suburbs, where each one is detached and there are few or no restrictions on aesthetics. Ushida Findlay have felt free to investigate geometries, plans, materials, and the sensitivities of clients without limiting their range with dogma. As they have written of Truss Wall, "rather than reinforce the shells that protect us, we must think of ourselves as open systems, taking in information from the outside while venturing outside ourselves – always in the interest of self-reform".

NEO-CLASSIC

Classicism is a thread running through 20th-century architecture, design, and decor just as it has influenced form for the last 2,500 years. From ancient Greece and the Parthenon, to the country houses in New England, to the prefabricated apartment blocks in the new Chinese cities of today, the canons of Classicism are all but impossible to ignore. In fact, the most considerable of the Modernists – Le Corbusier (see pp.18–9) and Mies Van der Rohe (see pp.20–1) among them – were avowedly indebted to the

Above The elements of Roman architecture are brought into the 20th century in a fresh manner by Joze Plecnik (1873–1957) in his austere kitchen in Ljubljana, Slovenia.

Right Neo-classic couture is seen here in the "Delphos" dress by Fortuny (1906).

Previous page (left)
This Paris apartment by Yves Gastou shows how Neo-classic design can be fused with Modernist elements to create a new, decorative synthesis.

Previous page (right)
The Fornasetti "Sun" chair (1955): lacquered and screen-printed moulded plywood – Louis XV for the mid-20th century.

architecture of ancient Greece. They saw themselves as extending the vocabulary of architecture or, perhaps, of pursuing Classicism by means other than the Doric, Ionic, and Corinthian Orders. The spirit and the style of Classicism has informed the 20th century as much as it did in previous eras. A part of the reason for this is the fact that Classical design is particularly adaptable. In this century it has been used to express the political and social values of Nazi Germany, Fascist Italy, and the Soviet Union. It has also been used to express the political and social values of the British Empire and the United States.

In Britain at the start of the 20th century there was a reaction against the excesses of the Arts and Crafts Movement, and this took the form of a return to the spirit of 18th-century building styles, applied to both domestic and public architecture. This, in turn, was to be influenced by a distinctly American brand of Neo-classicism that had become popular as a result of Daniel Burnham's grand plan for The World's Columbian Exposition in Chicago, Illinois, in 1893. This sprawling layout was known as "The White City" because of its preponderance of Classical white stucco buildings. The White City set the stage for the reinvention of two real cities. Burnham's replanning of Washington, D.C., in ·1901–2, and Chicago, in 1906–9, further entrenched an opulent American form of Neo-classicism, the most dazzling embodiments of which were, perhaps, the Pierpont Morgan Library in New York, built in 1903, and the original Pennsylvania Station, also in New York, built in 1910, both of which were designed by the influential architectural firm of McKim, Mead and White.

Neo-classicism has been played with by Pop designers and decorators, and turned upside down and back to front by Post-Modernists. It has been reinvented by oddball geniuses like Sir Edwin Lutyens (see pp.50–1), and continued as a singular style for housing all over the world. Think of Elvis Presley's Graceland, the Bishop's Avenue in London's Hampstead, or the Disney Corporation's all-American new town of Celebration, Florida. Consider Adolf Loos's 1922 Chicago Tribune Building entry – a vast inhabited Classical column – or Charles Moore's Piazza d'Italia in New Orleans (built in 1980, with U.I.G. and Perez Associates, Inc), where the five Classical Orders are reinvented as part of a complex archaeological and social narrative scenography. Think, too, of how on the drawing boards of other great architects, Classicism, stripped of all of its decoration – bull's heads, egg-and-dart, flutes, swags, triglyphs, and cornucopia – has been

transformed into some of the century's most powerful and most moving buildings, the former represented by, say, Giuseppe Terragni's Casa del Fascio in Como, Italy (see pp.54–5), and the latter by Gunnar Asplund's Forest Crematorium on the edge of Stockholm. Beyond its apparent chameleon-like character, Classicism has also represented the aspirations of clients for whom a home is not a real home, or not sufficiently grand, unless it sports at least a pediment or portico and maybe a run of pilasters or even full-blown columns, too. Over the course of the 20th century, such details have been reproduced in every material from stone to titanium via steel, fibreboard, and various plastics.

Above Sir Edwin Lutyens designed this table as a Neo-classical temple.

Below This covered walkway was designed by David Whitcomb for a 1980s house in New York State. The walls are concrete, not stone. The "altar" beneath the Old Master painting is a portable bar.

The social triumph of the business executive in the last two decades of the century, following the fall of Communism, encouraged a spate of pseudo-Classical housebuilding as new fortunes were made across the world. An architectural style that had symbolized the aspirations, virtues, and collective dreams of the Greek city and state has now come to serve those who made a success at private enterprise. And, as poor people in western and eastern cities began buying their own homes, they, too, aspired to Neo-classical design, calling for Neo-Georgian fanlight doors in Britain, concrete pediments in southern China, or fibreglass columns across America. Classicism was also used from the early years of the 20th century as a way of raising the tone of new forms of living, and especially of travelling. Trains, hotels, cars – particularly the Rolls Royce – and the most opulent ocean liners, were tricked out in classically inspired interiors before Modern design came into its own and was accepted as a style that could equally embody symbols of wealth, sophistication, and style.

By the end of the century, Modern design had all but triumphed and, despite the endeavours of Lutyens, Terragni, and Asplund, the Neo-classic had become debased. The new Classical temples were the glass houses designed by Philip Johnson and Mies van der Rohe, in which the spirit rather than the form of the ancient world was repossessed and represented in new materials stripped of the sheer weight of precedent and history.

Even so, there endures in the public perception (if not in the minds of the architectural élite) a powerful association between the most easily recognizable elements of Classical architecture and the popular notion of "class", which in this context denotes the sense of effortless sophistication.

Left *The style of the drawing room in the Viceroy's House is coolly monumental and derived from the work of Christopher Wren. The fireplace is on the scale of a war memorial.*

Right *The exotic design of the Viceroy's House's exterior gives way to a Modern play on English Baroque on the inside. The study is designed like one of Wren's ambitious City of London churches.*

EDWIN LUTYENS

PROFILE

BORN:

London, 1869 (d.1944)

EDUCATED:

Self-taught; worked for two years with the country-house architect Ernest George

PRINCIPAL COMMISSIONS:

Munstead Wood, Godalming Surrey, England, 1896

Deanery Garden, Sonning, Berkshire, England, 1899–1902

Nashdom, Taplow, Buckinghamshire, England, 1905–9

Viceroy's House, New Delhi, India, 1912–30

Britannic House, City of London, 1920–4

British Embassy, Washington, D.C., 1925–8

Midland Bank, City of London, 1924–39

Sir Edwin Lutyens began his prolific and influential career at the age of 20 with the first of a spate of superbly built country houses for the newly rich in the Home Counties of southern England. Early on, these were realized in an Arts and Crafts style. Lutyens pushed the style to creative limits (as at Deanery Gardens, see pp.6 and 8), before switching to an opulent and, if weighty, inventive Neo-classicism that ranged from excursions through the Baroque, to homages to Christopher Wren (what Lutyens called his "Wrenaissance" style), to remarkable Anglo-Indian fusions in New Delhi (Lutyens planned the new Indian imperial capital – it had moved from Calcutta, an earlier British-built city – from 1912).

Lutyens's genius was to take the Classical canons and make them his own. A playful architect who regarded architecture as a "high game," he makes you laugh quietly when you enter a room, because his architectural arrange-ments are genuinely witty. In the Viceroy's House (now the Rashtrapati Bhavan), there is a withdrawing room leading off the ballroom that boasts a full and richly decorated cornice and a deep-blue ceiling panel – or what appears to be one. In fact, the "panel" is simply the sky; it has been removed to let the heat out, but also to ensure that this (relatively) cool room is as elegant as the ballroom that the guests have just waltzed out of. Lutyens was an alchemist of existing styles rather than a direct influence on his contemporaries; his legacy was to carry 19th-century historicist design principles into the 20th century.

Left *The stairs, hall, and dining room of the Muller House, in Prague, flow as if one continuous space, a triumph of Modern meets Neo-classic homemaking. Note the rich materials. Loos was a master builder; his detailing is immaculate.*

Right *The circular lightwell with its wooden banisters brings daylight down the main stairs and into the heart of the Muller House.*

ADOLF LOOS

PROFILE

BORN:

Brno, Czech Republic, 1870 (d.1933)

EDUCATED:

National School of Arts and Crafts, Reichenberg, Germany

Technische Hochschule, Dresden, Germany

PRINCIPAL COMMISSIONS:

Kartner Bar, Vienna, 1907

Villa Stein, Vienna, 1910

Apartments and shops, Michaelerplatz, Vienna, 1910

Rufer House, Vienna, 1922

Tristan Tzara House, Paris, 1926

Moller House, Potzleinsdorf, Austria, 1928

Kuhner House, Payerbach, Austria, 1930

Muller House, Prague, 1930

Adolf Loos occupies a curious place in the development of Modern design, hovering solidly, but awkwardly, between a form of stripped Classicism and the Modernism that he advocated yet never really practised, except, perhaps, in the last of his great designs: the severe, rectilinear Muller House in Prague. Even then, one is always aware that no matter how formidable and chastening they might seem from the outside, Loos's houses are opulently and beautifully finished in rich, polished materials. What they do not indulge in, however, is decoration. In fact, Loos is best remembered as the first European architect to take a considered and consistent philosophical stance against decoration.

A stonemason's son (evident in the precision of the construction and finish of his buildings), he travelled extensively in the United States between 1893 and 1896, paying his way as a mason, floor-layer, and dishwasher. He was very much taken by Louis Sullivan's 1892 essay *Ornament in Architecture*, in which Sullivan, Frank Lloyd Wright's teacher, wrote: "It would be greatly for our esthetic good if we should refrain entirely from the use of ornament for a period of years, in order that our thought might concentrate acutely on the production of buildings well formed and comely in the nude." Loos's *Ornament and Crime* followed in 1908. Here the architect noted that the criminals in Vienna's jails were tattooed, evidence that ornament was criminal and should be eschewed.

ITALIAN RATIONAL STYLE

PROFILE

PRINCIPAL DESIGNERS:

Giuseppe Terragni, 1904–43

Adalberto Libera, 1903–63

Luigi Piccinato, 1899–1983

Curzio Malaparte, 1898–1957

PRINCIPAL COMMISSIONS:

Novocomum Apartment Block,
  Como, Italy, 1927–8

Casa del Fascio, Como, Italy,
  1932–6

Casa del Fascio, Lissone, Italy,
  1938–9

Sabaudia New Town,
  Sabaudia, Italy, c.1933

Casa Malaparte, Isle of Capri,
  Italy, 1942

"I am a reactionary and a revolutionary according to circumstance," said the Italian dictator Benito Mussolini. Much of the architecture commissioned when Mussolini was in power (1922–43) was a combination of stripped-down Roman Classicism and Modern Movement forms adopted from the Bauhaus (see pp.16–7). Italian Rationalism was in fact something of a balancing act between traditionally provincial styles and a revolutionary modernity. Socially driven, it was a style that came to inform the design of apartment buildings and houses as much as it did courts of justices, railway stations, Fascist Party headquarters, and even entire new towns such as the (still almost unchanged) Sabaudia.

At its best, this Rationalist style produced architecture and design of an extraordinarily high calibre. The finest public work in the style was Giuseppe Terragni's Casa del Fascio (now renamed the Casa del Popolo) in Como; the finest private commission was the house that Fascist writer Curzio Malaparte designed for himself (with considerable help from Adalberto Libera) on an all but inaccessible outcrop on the Isle of Capri. From the air, Casa Malaparte resembles a forgotten Roman amphitheatre, although what seem to be seats set in tiers are in fact steps leading up to the roof terrace – the first experience visitors have of this exquisite house. Below the terrace is the terracotta-coloured house itself. It incorporates cell-like bedrooms for guests and Malaparte's own extensive private rooms overlooking a particularly wonderful stretch of coastline and sea.

Casa Malaparte differs from the main body of designs in this style because it is a highly personal work; it was, said Malaparte, an image of his own nostalgia, or a representation of his life. The house has caught the imagination of successive generations of architects, designers, and homeowners, and it is undoubtedly one of the most beautiful and desirable houses in the world. This is surprising, because it is almost wholly free of decoration or soft surfaces, and yet it is awash with sunlight and hugs the rocks it stands on in a way that makes it seem as if it has been there forever.

This was part of the spirit that the Italian Rationalists were trying to engender in their work: a sense of timelessness and of natural, historic order. During this period the architects also designed schools, school furniture, and seaside holiday resorts for children that are still in use today.

In true Italian Rationalist style, the living room of the Casa Malaparte, on the Isle of Capri, Italy, designed by Curzio Malaparte and Adalberto Libera, is totally devoid of ornament, and bears no traces of traditional Mediterranean architecture.

Left The shell-pattern "wall panelling" of Piero Fornasetti's Italian dining room in his holiday villa bears his trademark of playful Modernism.

Right The design of Fornasetti's plates from his "Themes and Variations" series are distinctively surreal.

PIERO FORNASETTI

PROFILE

BORN:
Milan, Italy, 1923 (d.1988)

EDUCATED:
Academia Brera, Milan, Italy

PRINCIPAL COMMISSIONS:
"Acrobats" screen
"Boomerang" chair
"Themes and Variations"
  dinner plates
Ballroom of the Time-Life
  Building, 1963
Designs for ties, women's
  bathing suits, silk scarves,
  furniture, and lamps

The artist/designer Piero Fornasetti preferred to play witty games with the palette of art history rather than adopt what he saw as the dour tenets of abstract Modernism. Seemingly a Post-Modernist working 30 years too soon, Fornasetti decorated pianos, automobiles, plates, shops, boats, ashtrays, and umbrellas with his playful applications, stylistic dislocations, and surreal juxtapositions.

As a young man in Milan, Fornasetti was influenced by the painter Giorgio de Chirico, who opened Fornasetti's eyes to the possibilities of rearranging the Italian past in a playful Modern style. Fornasetti's style was unique: it was founded upon architectural perspectives and illusionism, and used a highly personal visual repertory of objects like playing cards, flowers, fish, and architectural details. Fornasetti's second great influence came in 1940, when he was introduced to then well-established architect/designer, Gio Ponti (see pp.64–5). They entered into a lasting collaboration, with Ponti providing the bewildering range of objects for Fornasetti to decorate with his exuberant cultural fragments.

By the mid-1950s Fornasetti had turned elegant whimsy into a light industrial process, employing 30 craftsmen to produce his designs. His Modern significance derives partly from his conviction that "something beautiful does not become less so, even when it is reproduced twenty or thirty thousand times". The preciousness of the unique art object held no interest for him, making it ironic that some items he produced are now very collectable. At the end of his life his work became passé and his commercial operation declined. Since his death, however, his fresh vision, love of craftsmanship, and prescient willingness to play elegant games with visual icons have cast him as a precursor of Modern design.

Left *Something old and something new: here David Hicks has redefined a Classical architectural interior with Modern-style objets, lighting, and furnishings to create a totally new look.*

DAVID HICKS

PROFILE

BORN:
London, 1929 (d.1999)

EDUCATED:
Central School of Arts and Crafts, London

PRINCIPAL COMMISSIONS:
Interiors from 1956 for:
Helena Rubinstein
The Prince of Wales
British Steel
Aeroflot
QEII (Cunard liner), 1969
Womenswear collections from
  1982

David Hicks stretched the legacy of the great American and British interior decorators from the middle to the end of the 20th century. His taste reflected a keen appreciation of developments in Modern architecture, yet was always informed by an equally developed love of Classical design, which he interpreted in new ways and often using new materials – plastic and Perspex (Plexiglas), for example – when these seemed appropriate or else enchanted him. He followed in the wake of a stately galleon of interior decorators led by Elsie de Wolfe (1856–1950) in New York, and Syrie Maugham (1879–1955) in London. Taken together, these designers represented a move away from fusty, cluttered interiors by those with taste and money, but for whom the radical aesthetic of the Bauhaus (see pp.16–7) and Le Corbusier (see pp.18–9) was simply too extreme. The Hicks look involved a tasteful mixing and matching of both antiques and custom-made furniture based on Classical designs. For decorating country houses he developed a style that often introduced powerful colours, like pinks and oranges, organized in bold geometric patterns to 18th-century designs. It was not unusual to find traditional rooms illuminated by Hicks with frankly modern light fittings.

Hicks was certainly Modern in the sense that he eschewed clutter, and not only made effective use of new materials and fabrics, but also of the latest lighting techniques. The overall effect was light, bright, and even a little shiny. But references to Classicism and Classical civilization were never far away – from his grand pedimented doors in living and dining rooms to his trademark marbleized or Perspex obelisks that graced desks and mantelshelves.

MID-CENTURY MODERN

Mid-century Modern: two words that have become more or less accepted as a specific style. Why? Because, in the aftermath of the Second World War, there emerged in the United States a highly recognizable new style of architecture and design that was very different in tone, spirit, and materials from European Modernism. If the experience of the Second World War had left Europe exhausted and prone to a form of navelgazing, witnessed in the tough and often graceless architectural styles such as the Brutalism that emerged in Britain during the austerity years of the early 1950s, the United States was running at full steam, spilling over with new industry, new ways of making things, with conviction and energy. The consumer boom that followed in the wake of Germany and Japan's defeat was reflected in the swish new buildings where consumer goods were designed and made, and in the style of a new wave of houses by those who profited by such goods either as manufacturers or buyers. What characterized this new wave of buildings that have never really gone out of fashion was their breathtaking self-confidence and sleek beauty. There were the California houses of Charles and Ray Eames (see pp.66–7) and of Pierre Koenig (see pp.68–9). There were the sleek office towers of Skidmore, Owings & Merrill (SOM) in New York and Chicago. There were the peerless designs of the General Motors Technical Center in Warren, Michigan (by Eliel Saarinen, with his son, Eero, see pp.38–9), and the West Point Military Academy in upstate New York. This was the architectural uniform of a self-confident nation, the richest the world had yet known, teetering on the edge of the space age – before the prolonged war in Vietnam and Cambodia dragged the United States down from the position of effortless, and by-and-large, unquestioned superiority it held in those remarkable years between 1945 and 1965.

The Mid-century Modern style was the product of several revolutions in taste and in methods of production in terms of materials and architectural design. The experience of the Second World War had pushed American industry to new heights. The defeat of Germany (if not Japan) was largely due to the inexhaustible supply of equipment from American factories. Mass-production techniques, including extensive prefabrication, were seen as a good thing rather than the enemy of tradition as they tended to be in Europe. In any event, American citizens had been used to the idea of buildings that could be erected quickly and even transported to a different site. The new architecture that made a virtue of these techniques, either in construction or aesthetically, was generally welcomed. The Eameses and Koenig transformed the methods of prefabrication and factory-produced materials into canonic works of art.

Below *Case Study House No. 22, designed by Pierre Koenig in 1959, is representative of laid-back California living in a wonderfully graceful glass-and-steel construction.*

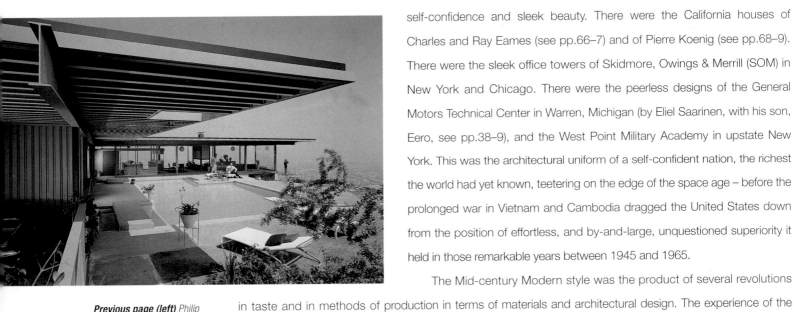

Previous page (left) *Philip Johnson's Glass House, built in 1949 in New Canaan, Connecticut, is a prism in a park-like landscape.*

Previous page (right) *This mobile by the American sculptor Alexander Calder is made of steel wire and sheet aluminium. Its biomorphic shapes move naturally, and are infinitely responsive to their environment.*

A second revolution occured in the way that architecture was made. At this time, there emerged a new type of architectural company that could match and mirror the slickness and professionalism of big business. The firm of SOM, founded in 1936, had from the beginning adopted the organizational principles and corporate culture of the American business world, practising stringent economic working methods while promoting teamwork, motivation, and individual responsibility. The result was that, by the time SOM built the Lever House in New York in 1952, it was able to project itself as a new-style architectural firm, gaining international recognition with stylistically dazzling buildings while operating like serious businessmen.

The third revolution that spurred the Mid-century Modern look was the one caused by the arrival in the United States of such key European talents as Walter Gropius and Mies van der Rohe (see pp.20–1). It was Mies in particular who showed how high art and big business could slip happily into one another's shoes. "Mies means money", said North American businessmen as they watched with admiration as the super-smooth Seagram Building (1958) rose on New York's Park Avenue. This was a style of architecture that dovetailed with the emergence of a self-confident new wave of furniture by, among others, Charles and Ray Eames, Harry Bertoia, Isamu Noguchi, and George Nelson (see pp.74–5). If there was a European branch of Mid-century Modern, it is seen at its best in the all-embracing work of the Danish architect and designer Arne Jacobsen (see pp.70–1).

In the end, Mid-century Modern was at heart American and it was as much a stance as a style. For those who believed that the Modern Movement, for all its formal virtues, had introduced an essentially alien European style to an exuberant America, the work of Charles and Ray Eames, Koenig, SOM, and their contemporaries gave weight to the idea that a confident "can-do" America could celebrate both its energy and strength in ways that did not always have to be imported.

Above The soaring United States Airforce Academy chapel in Colorado exemplifies the post-World War II American architectural confidence that here links the military and the spiritual.

Left Arne Jacobsen's "Ant" chair, Model No. 3100 (1953), designed for Fritz Hansen, is a Mid-century Modern design classic.

Left This is the main living room of the highly theatrical Villa Planchart in Caracas, Venezuela. Ponti, who designed every detail, described the house as "a butterfly alighted on the top of a hill", and its richly decorated interior as a "fugue of natural and artificial perspectives".

GIO PONTI

PROFILE

BORN:

Milan, Italy, 1891 (d.1979)

EDUCATED:

Milan Polytechnic,
Milan, Italy

PRINCIPAL COMMISSIONS:

Catholic Press Exhibition,
Vatican City, Italy, 1936

Offices for Monescatini, Milan,
Italy, 1938/1951

Villa Planchart, Caracas,
Venezuela, 1955

Pirelli Tower, Milan, Italy,
1958

Parco dei Principi Hotel,
Sorrento, Italy, 1960

Denver Art Museum, Denver,
Colorado, 1971

Founder and Editor of *Domus*
magazine, Milan, Italy, 1928

Furniture designer, best known
for "Superleggera" chair,
Cassina, Italy, 1957

Fabric design, glassware, and
ceramics

The godfather of Modern Italian design, Gio Ponti led the great post-World War II renaissance in Italian design and manufacturing from his home town of Milan. In 1928, Ponti founded *Domus*, a magazine devoted to promoting Modern design in all its forms, from fabrics to furniture to office blocks. Yet, in Ponti's eyes, Modern design had little to do with Le Corbusier's "machine for living" (see pp.18–9) and everything to do with beauty, variety, and sensuality. In this sense, alone, he was very much ahead of his time: his work and inspiration looked forward to the 1970s and 1980s, when the rest of Modern architecture and design finally caught up with him.

A good deal of Ponti's work is playful, and some of it is plain funny. His two most famous works – the "Superleggera" chair for Cassina (1957) and the Pirelli office tower (1958), which greets visitors arriving in Milan by train – are serious designs, yet both make use of subtle curves and have a lightness of touch missing in much of the design of the time.

Ponti's influence was to have a significant effect not so much on his contemporaries, but rather on the generation that included Ettore Sottsass (see pp.128–9) and Alessandro Mendini, who created the Milan design studios Memphis and Studio Alchymia (see pp.120–3) that caused such a stir on the international scene from the end of the 1970s with their irreverent approach to furniture, interiors, and ultimately to architecture. If they pushed the fight against the restricted and puritanical too far, Ponti's work remained as an enduring guide of how Modern design can create warm and witty work without getting caught in the web of just another new fashion or dogma.

Left The generous scale
of the Eames House was
made possible by the use
of low-cost, prefabricated
components. The factory-like
character of the architecture
is offset by soft furnishings,
plants, flowers, antiques,
and American memorabilia.

Right Charles and Ray Eames
at home. Note the famous
lounge chair and attendant
ottoman: they look as good in
a home as they do in an office.

CHARLES & RAY EAMES

PROFILES

CHARLES EAMES

BORN:

St Louis, Missouri, 1907 (d.1978)

EDUCATED:

Washington University School
of Architecture, St Louis,
Missouri

RAY EAMES

BORN:

New York, 1912 (d.1988)

EDUCATED:

Cranbrook Academy of
Art, Bloomfield Hills, Michigan

PRINCIPAL COMMISSIONS:

Moulded plywood chairs for
  Evans Wood Products, 1946
Eames House, Pacific
  Palisades, California, 1949
Lounge chair and ottoman for
  Herman Miller, New York, 1956

Charles and Ray Eames lived out a Modern domestic dream. In 1949, they designed their own house near Los Angeles, built of factory components. Far from cold and inhuman, its technological frame was set among beautiful trees, while inside Ray decorated it with superb fabrics, plants, objects, and primitive antiques that gave it the warmth, colour, and sensual qualities that many Modern architects' houses lacked. By dovetailing their talents – Charles for design, Ray for decoration – they produced a body of work that has remained in vogue ever since.

Charles had two collaborators and mentors – the architect Eero Saarinen (see pp.38–9) and the designer George Nelson (see pp.74–5) – who brought him into the public eye with exhibitions of his innovative furniture in New York in 1940 and 1946. Eames's office furniture is as desirable now (for both the home and the office) as it was in the 1950s and 1960s, and his most famous design was a leather-and-rosewood lounge chair and ottoman made as a one-off in 1955 for the film director Billy Wilder. Along with Breuer's "Bauhaus" chair it became an international icon of Modern style. The 1958 "Aluminum" chair shared its construction principles with Eames's seating for Chicago's O'Hare and Washington's Dulles airports. The Eameses combined natural materials – principally leather – with aluminium and other lightweight alloys to create beautifully realized products and designs that always said "high quality" in both their visual and tactile finishes.

Left The crystal-clear design and construction of Case Study House No. 21, is seen here when the house was brand new. The surrounding pool gives the house the feel of a modern Japanese pavilion.

Right This is easy Modern living the Mid-century way. The furniture is the very latest by Nelson and Eames. The housewife is a fashion model; the man about the house is Pierre Koenig himself.

PIERRE KOENIG

PROFILE

BORN:
San Francisco, California, 1925

EDUCATED:
University of Utah School of Engineering, Utah
Pasadena City College, Pasadena, California
University of California, Los Angeles, California

PRINCIPAL COMMISSIONS:
Own house, Los Angeles, California, 1950
Case Study House No. 21, Los Angeles, California, 1958
Case Study House No. 22, Los Angeles, California, 1959
Own house, Los Angeles, California, 1985
Schwartz House, Pacific Palisades, California, 1994–6

Although superficially similar to the glass-and-steel houses of Mies van der Rohe (see pp.20–1) at Plano, Illinois, the much-celebrated Case Study houses of Pierre Koenig were designed to be built at the lowest possible cost from readily available factory-made components. Koenig's hope was that such light and graceful houses could be mass-produced for California's less well-off buyers. This never happened. Instead, Koenig's classic Mid-century Modern homes have become fashionable and are sought after by those with taste and money.

Since he was a student at UCLA, Koenig has always lived in glass and steel of his own design. The most perfect, if not the grandest or most dramatic, is Case Study House No. 21 (it was one of a number of houses commissioned by *Arts and Architecture* magazine to show what a new and affordable California house might be in the 1950s). Although its construction is simple – sheer glass sheets fixed between black-painted steel I-beams – the design is extremely subtle. The house stands surrounded by a geometric pool of water. As well as creating gentle reflections, the pool water is pumped over the steel roof to keep it cool, returning to the pool through chutes that chuckle gently throughout the heat of the day. The house has been used as a symbol of the clean, transparent, democratic new world between 1945 and the early 1960s.

Left The living room of Jacobsen's own home shows the balance of formal and relaxed design. The room, furniture, fabrics, and lamps are all up-to-the-minute, yet the atmosphere is relaxed.

Right The dining table and high-backed chairs in the Hall of St Catherine's College, Oxford, display Jacobsen's superb craftsmanship.

ARNE JACOBSEN

PROFILE

BORN:

Copenhagen, 1902 (d.1971)

EDUCATED:

Royal Danish Academy of Arts, Copenhagen

PRINCIPAL COMMISSIONS:

Bellavista Estate, Copenhagen, 1934

Stelling House, Copenhagen, 1937

Town Hall, Aarhus, Sweden, 1937

Town Hall, Sollerod, Sweden, 1940–2

Jespersen Offices, Copenhagen, 1955

SAS Building, Copenhagen, 1958–60

St Catherine's College, Oxford, England, 1960–4

City Hall, Mainz, Germany, 1970–3

National Bank, Copenhagen, 1961–71

Jacobsen was that rare creature in the story of Modernism – a craftsman at heart who embraced the Modern project wholeheartedly while remaining true to his Arts and Crafts roots. He is as much revered for the highly original and sculptural silverware he designed for Georg Jensen as he is for the design of fabrics and inventive plywood furniture. Danish architects were trained, as many still are, as all-round designers for whom a building is an all-embracing work of art. At its most extreme, as in the case of St Catherine's College, Oxford – a mid-century masterpiece – the sense of everything being designed by one man can be a little overwhelming. Because the college is an artwork, it seems a curious home for students, who might have preferred a looser-reined environment.

Nevertheless, Jacobsen's interiors are beautifully made, simple, light, and well proportioned. His work is all the more interesting in that it reflects not only the influence of the great 20th-century Swedish Classicist, Gunnar Asplund, but also that of Mies van der Rohe (see pp.20–1). In Jacobsen is found the spirit of Classicism, the Arts and Crafts, and his era's latest curtain walling and steely office blocks. His buildings have stood the test of time; his silverware is as fashionable now as it was in the early 1960s. Jacobsen also designed notable chairs for Fritz Hansen: the "Ant" chair (1953), and the "Egg" and "Swan" chairs – the latter two first appearing in 1958 at Copenhagen's SAS Hotel. These have become the recognizable icons of Jacobsen's broad style: a brand of Danish Modern fusing together equal parts of visual élan and technical sophistication.

Left *Looking out over the Hollywood Hills from the Chemosphere – the house appears to float in space, a sensation heightened by the wrap-around windows and lofty open-plan living space.*

Right *Lautner's homes are both rooted in the landscape and opened up to it. This is the inside-outside living room of the Reiner House, known as "Silver Top".*

JOHN LAUTNER

PROFILE

BORN:

Marquette, Michigan, 1911
(d.1995)

EDUCATED:

Taliesin, with Frank Lloyd
Wright

PRINCIPAL COMMISSIONS:

Lautner House, Los Angeles,
 California, 1940
Carling Residence, Los
 Angeles, California, 1947
Pearlman House, Idyllwild,
 California, 1957
Malin Residence,
 Los Angeles, California, 1960
Reiner House, Los Angeles,
 California, 1963
Elrod Residence, Palm Springs,
 California, 1979
Sheats/Goldstein House, Los
 Angeles, California, 1963–89

"The only absolute," wrote John Lautner, in architecture as in life, "is Change-Growth-Life." Lautner was one of the star graduates of Frank Lloyd Wright's Taliesin Winter Camp in Arizona, which the young architect literally helped to build in the 1930s. Lautner, however, although influenced by Wright, went on to create a domestic architecture that was more emphatically futuristic, emerging from his mentor's shadow to create a very individual architectural aesthetic that always seemed most at home in Southern California. He was a polemicist who railed against what he saw as the tyranny of the architecture of rules and 90-degree angles. He approached the design of each of the often-spectacular houses in his portfolio as unique projects. If his houses have anything in common, it is the easy flow of internal space and the soaring roofs that enclose that space.

Lautner's most famous design, built for a young aircraft engineer who wanted to live high in the sky, is the Malin Residence. Known as the Chemosphere, it sprouts from a Hollywood hillside. The house, 18 metres (60 feet) in diameter with all-around views, springs from a tall, 3.5-metre (12-foot) diameter concrete column which contains all of the essential services. Isolated like an eagle's nest – although it looks more like a UFO from a 1950s Hollywood movie – the house is reached by an electrically powered cable car. The windows of the Chemosphere are angled back to avoid creating a sense of vertigo – which would be induced easily in visitors if they could look straight down the precipitous hillside.

Left *George Nelson's schemes were based around the notion of "open plan" living – with multifunctional furniture increasing the sense of space.*

Right *Nelson's "Marshmallow" sofa (1956) consisted of foam-filled circular pads backed with steel discs, on a painted tubular steel frame.*

GEORGE NELSON

PROFILE

BORN:
Hartford, Connecticut, 1908
(d.1986)

EDUCATED:
Yale University, New Haven,
Connecticut
Catholic University of America,
Washington, D.C.
American Academy in Rome

PRINCIPAL COMMISSIONS:
Fairchild House, New York,
1941
"Storagewall" shelving for
Herman Miller, New York, 1944
Herman Miller showrooms,
1948–64
"Marshmallow" sofa for
Herman Miller, New York, 1956
Loeb Student Center interiors,
New York University, 1959
Chrysler Pavilion, New York
World's Fair, 1964
AO2 Action Office for Herman
Miller, 1968

As a teacher, writer, editor, designer, and architect, George Nelson played a hugely important role in the development of American design in the aftermath of the Second World War. He clearly showed how the mass-production methods and new materials created during the war could be linked to bright colours and even brighter ideas. The furniture systems he created for Herman Miller (with Henry Wright and Robert Propst) revolutionized the office interior. From now on the wall could become not just a division between one room and another, but also a cupboard or shelving system. His furniture was often genuinely funny (the "Marshmallow" sofa is a good example and remains a perennial favourite among designers and design buffs).

Tomorrow's House, the book Nelson published with Henry Wright in 1945, was a clarion call for a new way of open-plan living: lightweight furniture, furniture that could serve several functions, and the maximum use of space from the smallest home. This seems commonplace now, yet it was a radical idea at the time. He believed in breaking down barriers between the art and design worlds, and forecast with great accuracy the way we would work at home as much as in the office, as changes took place in business corporations which he himself helped to revolutionize. He has been a proactive figure in the design world, not only as the visionary creator of The "Action" Office (1965) for Herman Miller (an early ergonomic perspective on the office environment) but also as a journalist, and his work for the International Design Conference at Aspen, Colorado.

OSCAR NIEMEYER

PROFILE

BORN:

Rio de Janeiro, Brazil, 1907

EDUCATED:

Escola Nacional de Belas-
Artes, Rio de Janeiro, Brazil

PRINCIPAL COMMISSIONS:

Ministry of Education
and Health, Rio de Janeiro,
1937–43

Yacht Club, Pampulha,
Brazil, 1943–4

Church of Sao Francisco,
Pampulha, Brazil, 1946

Architect's own home, 1953

Supreme Court, Brasília, 1958

Congress Buildings, Brasília,
1958

Presidential Palace, Brasília,
1958

Brasília Cathedral, 1970

House of Culture, Le
Havre, France, 1972

Oscar Niemeyer brought great sensuality to chaste Modern architecture. His inspiration, he said, was the mountain views around Rio, the ocean, the beaches, and the beautiful women that lay on them. This may be considered sexist today, yet there is no doubt that Niemeyer introduced a powerful and desirable female element into the essentially masculine concrete architecture of the mid-century. His buildings have great sculptural qualities, and each is such a daring and even shocking structure that it is impossible not to react strongly to them. In this sense they are often "one-liners", buildings that are best seen from some distance as artworks in the landscape. This is not to say that their interiors disappoint – they don't – but that Niemeyer injected four-square Modern architecture with a Latin theatricality and a sensibility that might be described as Baroque.

His first major project was the design of the Ministry of Education and Health building, which he worked on with Le Corbusier (see pp.18–9) during the latter's short stay in Brazil in 1936. In the years that followed he adopted ever more experimental and sculptural forms. His greatest work was to plan the new Brazilian capital, Brasília, between 1957 and 1979, and to design its major buildings, including a cathedral in the guise of a crown of thorns. His own house and studio overlooking Copacabana beach are quite breathtaking, opening out to the landscape like some exotic flower. His work has lost none of its sculptural or imaginative power even from our current vantage point.

*The astonishing space-station-
like interior of the House of
Culture, Le Havre, France,
features distinctive Niemeyer
chairs. The great sculptural
sweep of the interior is typical
of the architect's work.*

Left *The living room and kitchen of the Rose Seidler House is a hollowed-out cube filled with light and built of enduring materials. The stone anchors the house in the landscape, while furnishings and fittings are light and airy.*

Right *In the main bedroom, design is minimized; daylight and tactile materials create a sense of visual warmth.*

HARRY SEIDLER

PROFILE

BORN:

Vienna, 1923

EDUCATED:

Cambridge Technical College, Cambridge, England

University of Manitoba, Canada

Harvard University, Cambridge, Massachusetts

Black Mountain College, Beria, North Carolina, studying under Joseph Albers

PRINCIPAL COMMISSIONS:

Rose Seidler House, Sydney, NSW, 1948–50

Seidler House, Killara, Sydney, 1966–7

Meares House, Birchgrove, Sydney, 1994–5

Riverside Centre, Brisbane, Queensland, 1983–6

IBM Tower, Darling Park, Sydney, 1990–1

Grollo Tower, Melbourne, 1995–2000

Although born in Austria, Harry Seidler trained in England, the United States, and Canada. He worked with Alvar Aalto (see pp.22–3), Marcel Breuer (1902–81), and Oscar Niemeyer (see pp.76–7), before settling in Sydney, where he became Australia's best-known architect.

An indefatigable Modernist, Seidler has never turned his back on the Bauhaus (see pp.16–7) and the Corbusian (see pp.18–9) roots of the Modern Movement. His houses of the late 1940s and early 1950s echo the lyrical Rationalism of his teacher Breuer's work of the same period. By the 1960s he was winning larger-scale commissions, and his many office towers show no hint of Post-Modern influence. While these skyscrapers are rigorous in a severe manner, his houses are of altogether softer designs, imbued with subtle curves and interplays of interlocking spaces. Given the sunny climate of New South Wales, Seidler's houses are designed to open up as much as possible to the landscape and the light. If they sometimes appear to be rigorously geometric – and they are – this geometry is often broken up by internal courtyards and stairs that move balletically through the houses, creating varied and artful views both internally and externally.

Given that, in 1995, Seidler began working on the ambitious, highly sophisticated and spectacular skyscraper, the Grollo Tower, designed to thrust Melbourne into the new millennium, it seems almost ironic that the architect's first house (the Rose Seidler House) is an historic monument open to the public.

POP

Pop art and Pop music had kicked in some time before the phenomenon we like to label Pop affected architecture and design. It was, however, only a question of time. Perhaps it's possible to look at two strands of Pop design: the commercial and the cultural. The two are intertwined, and yet there is a big and recognizable divide between, say, the Pop philosophy of Archigram (in London),Superstudio (in Florence), and the young Hans Hollein (in Vienna). Concurrently with these there was also the

Below *The conversation pit typified the concerns of the new Pop order to redefine not just our built environment but our social habits as well.*

explosion of zany boutiques, clubs, bars, conversation pits, trip boxes, The Beatles' *Sergeant Pepper's Lonely Hearts Club Band* album with Peter Blake's Pop art cover, London's theatrical Biba department store, and the psychedelic alternative press. Significantly, the driving force of the new Pop culture was almost exclusively British. Previously, Britain and much of Europe had always copied the looks and manners of American youth culture heroes, but here the process was reversed: America's response to

The Beatles was The Monkees, a prefabricated group no more authentic than Euro-Elvis clones of the 1950s like Johnny Halliday or Cliff Richard.

At one level, there was a serious side to Pop: Pop produced surprisingly substantial artworks from Andy Warhol's Factory in New York, for example, and it generated the influential architectural fantasies of Archigram that led, eventually, to buildings like Richard Rogers' Pompidou Centre (see pp.100–1) in the next decade. Pop, then, had a life beyond Andy Warhol's "15 minutes" (the Pop era, he said, was one in which everybody would be famous for 15 minutes). By connecting a vibrant new culture that had grown out of Rock'n'Roll to the established arts – painting, sculpture, architecture – Pop expanded from The Beatles' *She Loves You* and Mary Quant's mini-skirts to cultural centres a decade on, via radical new approaches to the design of furniture and interiors. These included the experimental use of new materials, the inspirational film sets of Stanley Kubrick's *2001: A Space Odyssey*, the excesses of Post-Modernism on the one hand and a sensual, soft New Modernism on the other. In other words, Pop mattered. It held universal appeal and was, on the whole, Modern in its sensibilities.

Below right *The textured "Quaderna" table from the late 1960s is by the Italian experimental group Superstudio.*

Previous page (left) *The Love Shack, much used in videos, is the quintessential Pop interior.*

Previous page (right) *The "Panton" chair, designed by Verner Panton in 1959, set the fashion for injection-moulded construction, although the first model was actually made of polyurethane hard foam.*

In the story of architecture there have been two Pop groups: Archigram and Superstudio. Archigram, it's often said, did for architecture what The Beatles did for Pop music. The group was composed of young architects trained at the Architectural Association, in London, who found themselves working together. They launched a magazine, *Archigram*, and put on an exhibition for new forms and ways of Pop living, "Living City", at the Institute of Contemporary Arts, in London, in 1963. Archigram's projects (none of them built and few of them buildable) were demonstrations of how people might live freer, brighter, and less conventional lives than they had in traditional, historic cities if they were to embrace new forms of liberating technology. So, Ron Herron dreamed up a wonderful "Walking City" (1964) that could go wherever its citizens wanted it to go. Peter Cook

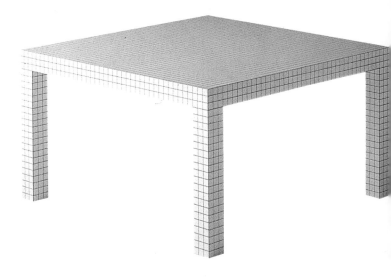

devised a "Plug-In City" (1966) that could be added to *ad infinitum*. There were designs for instant cities, inflatable homes, and space-age living pods. It was all tremendous fun, yet quite serious, and – beneath a surface of slick and clever, cartoon-like drawings – influential.

In Florence, Superstudio (1966–78) proposed subversive designs as a critique of Modern architecture and the Modern city. They planned to flood the whole of Florence; only Brunelleschi's dome would rise above the waters of the new Superstudio Aquatic Centre. At the same time, the group collaborated on the design of inflatable furniture and other wacky pieces that have since become collectors' items. Having run out of ideas to subvert, Superstudio disbanded in the late 1970s.

Elsewhere, Pop design knocked the stuffing out of starchy interiors. Set designers were able to spread new ideas for fashion, furniture, and home decor through radical Pop TV programs, such as British commercial television's highly original series *The Avengers* and *The Prisoner*. Both were showcases of Pop design and *The Avengers* in particular delighted in contrasting traditional British stereotypes with subversive symbols of the Swinging Sixties. The approach was carried through into the early James Bond movies, also copied without much conviction in America with movies such as *In Like Flint* (1967), and rather more stylishly in France with de Broca's *L'Homme de Rio* (1964).

Much of Pop design was ephemeral, yet that was what it had to be: a product of the fast-moving cycle of fashion, Pop design had to die before it got old. However, after the burial, British Pop lived on, having greatly influenced designers like Ettore Sottsass (see pp.128–9) and Elio Fiorucci. Pop showed what was possible, and its example was to influence both Post-Modernism and the Crafts Revival. Its legacy was the democratization of design, suggesting to more people than ever before that design could give you not what you needed, but what you wanted.

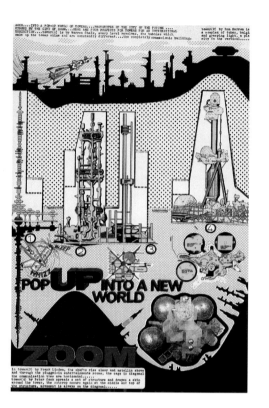

Left A poster for Archigram, the 1960s social agitators who believed in architecture by drawing, and who coalesced after their 1963 "Living City" exhibition at London's Institute of Contemporary Arts.

Below Inflatable furniture was unheard of before the late 1960s, when the Italian team of De Pas, D'Urbino, and Lomazzi designed the first completely pneumatic plastic chair. Manufactured by Zanotta, it typified Pop's delight in rendering traditionally solid and durable objects lightweight and transitory.

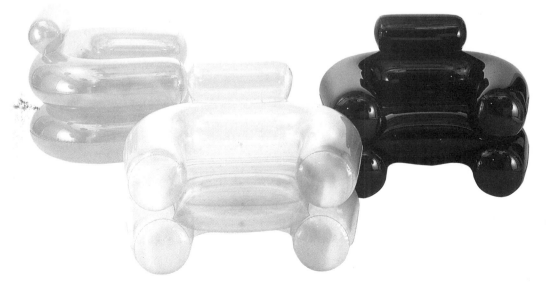

Left *This exhibition installation in Zurich, Switzerland, features Panton's innovative "Stacking" chair (1960): the first single-material, single-form injection-moulded chair to be produced.*

Right *As a great advocate of synthetic materials, always brightly coloured, Panton challenged people's perceptions of what furniture should be.*

VERNER PANTON

PROFILE

BORN:
Gamtofte, Denmark, 1926
(d.1999)

EDUCATED:
Technical School, Odense,
Denmark
Royal Academy of Fine Arts,
Copenhagen

PRINCIPAL COMMISSIONS:
"Cone" chair for Plus Linje, 1957
"Heart" chair for Fritz Hansen,
   1959
"Stacking" chair for
   Vitra/Herman Miller, 1960
   (in production from 1967)
"Living Tower" furniture for
   Herman Miller, 1969
"Panthella" lamps for Louis
   Poulsen, 1970
Fabrics for Mira-X from 1969
Numerous exhibition stands

"The main purpose of my work," wrote Verner Panton, "is to provoke people into using their imaginations. Most people spend their lives in dreary gray-beige conformity, mortally afraid of using colours. By experimenting with lighting, colours, textiles, and furniture and utilizing the latest technologies, I try to show new ways to encourage people to use their fantasy and make their surroundings more exciting."

Panton – certainly a colourful designer – settled in Switzerland in 1963 after spells with Arne Jacobsen (see pp.70–1) in Copenhagen and as a free-lance architect and designer in France. He enjoyed creating room settings and "environments", mostly in exhibitions and showrooms, that challenged visitors to rethink what furniture and the home might be. His furniture and lighting designs were highly sculptural and immense fun, and he was a great believer in synthetic materials and their sculptural possibilities. He also made sophisticated and rational use of new technologies: Panton's "Stacking" chair (see p.81) was the first one-piece, injection-moulded, cantilevered chair to be made. Its method of production was the stuff of men in white laboratory coats, yet the result was a design that never fails to raise a smile: clever and stylish, it can be seen everywhere from cafés in Havana to architects' offices in Canton, China.

Left This "Rotoliving" unit (1969) was installed in Colombo's apartment in Milan. The bedroom is hidden behind a corrugated sweep of curtains. Flexibility was the key, but the curtain is also sculptural.

Right In the bedroom (seen from the living-dining-kitchen area), the bed is like a High-Tech tent; it can be folded away just as the bedroom can.

JOE COLOMBO

PROFILE

BORN:

Milan, Italy, 1930 (d.1971)

EDUCATED:

Brera Academy of Fine Art, Milan, Italy

Milan Polytechnic, Milan, Italy

PRINCIPAL COMMISSIONS:

Interiors, Continental Hotel, Sardinia, 1964

"Universale" chair for Kartell, 1965

"Spider" lamp, 1965

"Tube" chair, 1969

"Rotoliving" unit, 1969

"Boby" trolley for Kartell, 1970

"Total Furnishing Unit", 1971

Although a promising painter, sculptor, and architect, the precocious Joe (born Cesare) Colombo made his name in a brief and dazzling career as a Milan-based designer of sophisticated furniture, ingenious lighting, and futuristic living spaces. The latter, such as the "Rotoliving" unit (1969), contained several functions, and were intended to be mass-produced and plugged into houses to provide an all-in-one High-Tech kitchen, bedroom, and bathroom to update old apartments.

He was not, however, a cold, Rationalist designer, but rather one of great exuberance. Whatever he turned his hand to, from a hostess trolley to a table-top lamp to seating, was always witty and imaginatively sculpted. In this sense, Colombo linked the arts of architect, painter, sculptor, and industrial designer very effectively. His exploitation of plastic, elevating it to a sophisticated and multi-functional material, has inspired designers in Europe and the United States ever since. He was keen to make things for the home that most people could afford, but – ironically – production and marketing costs made this difficult. His designs became cult objects almost as they appeared and they reach unimaginable prices in auction rooms today. To try to reduce costs, Colombo made extensive use of new materials: his "Spider" lamp (1965) was the first to use the then-new halogen bulb; the "Elda" chair (1963) was the first large armchair to be made wholly of fibreglass; and his "Universale" stacking chair (1965) was one of the first attempts to make a plastic injection-moulded chair in a single piece.

SWINGING LONDON

Many of Pop's most vigorous stirrings emanated from the neighbourhoods of London. Movies like *Blow-Up* (1965) spread the imagery of Swinging London's iconoclastic revolt into style, but it was the American Richard Lester who directed the definitive word. In *Help!* (1965) The Beatles walk through four adjacent front doors in a drab street of terraced houses and enter a large, single interior white space, the antithesis of the cramped parlours the exterior promised. In *The Knack* (1965) a pot of white paint is used to transform a dingy post-war London domestic interior into a palace of cool. Out with the old, in with the new.

In London's Chelsea, Terence Conran dreamed up the retail outlet Habitat, providing a whole generation with a stylish and affordable alternative to their parents' type of furniture. In Kensington, Barbara Hulanicki launched her Biba boutiques, which eventually coalesced into the Biba department store, a citadel of Art Nouveau, Art Deco, and Victorian kitsch.

London-based architects like Max Clendinning left the staid firm of Sir John Brown, A.E. Henson & Partners to set up their own practices and design radical houses and interiors for clients newly liberated by the Zeitgeist. Also helping to define the times were Archigram (see pp.81–3 and p.94) and Cedric Price, a radical architect practising in London since 1960 and a lifelong champion of temporary, mobile, recyclable, and adaptable buildings. Price, an influential theorist, challenged the notion of buildings as monuments, advocating instead structures responsive to society's needs – an idea perfectly in tune with the 1960s and one that influenced a generation of architects.

Out with the old and in
with the new: the style of
Swinging London was in
complete contrast to the
dreary post-war architecture
and furnishings. White-
painted walls, caterpillar-
like beanbag seating,
organic-style lighting
(as seen in this London
apartment by Max Clendinning)
all epitomized the era.

Left Seating (by Eero Saarinen, 1955) is at the heart of Villa Spies's plastic dome. The seats rise when the dining pod pushes up from the floor below. The plastic pod at the back has a multi-function service unit.

Right The layers of the house open up like a flower: the multi-function service unit and bedroom are on display; the conversation pit is to the left.

STAFFAN BERGLUND

PROFILE

BORN:
Stockholm, Sweden, 1936

EDUCATED:
Royal Institute of Technology, Stockholm
University of Wisconsin, Wisconsin, USA

PRINCIPAL COMMISSIONS:
Villa Spies, near Stockholm, 1969

Berglund's Villa Spies owes some of its inspiration to Frank Lloyd Wright (see pp.36–7) and the NASA space program, yet it is also a unique one-off that captures the spirit of its time. Berglund achieved this by linking Pop to space imagery and technology to create a house that is inventive, playful, and practical. The idea was developed from a competition Berglund won to design the ideal holiday villa for the Swedish travel entrepreneur Simon Spies; Spies liked the idea so much that he had Berglund build him a weekend retreat based on the same principles. Whether in housing or commercial interiors, Berglund creates spaces in which we can play-act our lives, rather than be serious all the time.

Tucked into rocks on a stretch of the Stockholm archipelago, the Villa Spies is a circular house – a plastic dome capping a concrete base. The house is on two levels. On top is one large circular room that opens onto a patio and bowl-like swimming pool. Plastic pods around the top space open up to reveal the bedroom, bathroom, and a service area. Guests sit in a conversation pit before and after meals: when meals are ready, they appear at the touch of a button in a circular dining pod that rises from the centre of the room. (Down below is a kitchen and guest area.) Around the room are more than 20 speakers which convey music and recordings of natural sounds; the colour of this white room can be changed by lamps hanging from a steel ring in the dome's centre. These also project images – from slides – around the space.

HIGH-TECH

This form of design has many roots, some of them new, others dating back a century and a half. What High-Tech styling seemed to prove was that the industrial age had matured to the point whereby, far from being fearful of machines and the image of the machine, people had grown not just used to them, but fond of them. The terrible images in Fritz Lang's *Metropolis*, in which the wretched of the earth are condemned to live in some demonic subterranean world where

Below At the steely bar at Legend's nightclub, in London, by Eva Jiricna (1986), the cladding of the columns resembles cheese graters, without being as sharp.

Right In the "Robo-Stacker" cabinet by Jam, a London design team, the metal base and glass top sandwich four steel drums used for washing machines.

Previous page (left)
Michael Hopkins designed this High-Tech bedroom for his London home.

Previous page (right)
Achille and Pier Giacomo Castiglioni's High-Tech "Mezzadro" stool (1957) has a lacquered seat, chromed-steel legs, and beech footrest.

they feed the insatiable machines that drive the world of wealth, luxury, and power above them, had lost their power to frighten. It is significant that just as High-Tech design became fashionable, so the age of heavy-duty industry that had inspired it, at one level, was coming to an end. In a sense, High-Tech design was a fond farewell to a passing era, and was as much a memorial as a celebration of a past way of making things. As if to emphasize this, it is interesting to note that the majority of the best High-Tech buildings have been all but hand-crafted. It has always been far simpler during the 20th century to erect a large building quickly using poured concrete or steel frames: High-Tech architecture, being more elaborate, required real skills and as much individual handicraft as an airliner does.

The reason for this was that because High-Tech often proposed novel design solutions, many components had to be manufactured specially. Technical solutions cumulatively developed over decades were suddenly abandoned, research and development was starting to take place on a project-by-project basis, and whole new sub-disciplines evolved. These often arose from the design and manufacturing problems associated with glass curtain walls. Norman Foster's 1995 Willis Faber Building (see pp.102–3) not only proposed rigorous new specifications for glass panels (specifications only reluctantly met at the last minute by suppliers loath to guarantee more than they had to), but also involved the design and refinement of sophisticated patch fittings that permitted vertical movement of glass panes without horizontal shifting. The same building was given extensive under-floor cabling provisions in a prescient building design initiative that was soon to save the tenant large sums of money but for which there was no real precedent in the early 1970s.

The more theatrical aspects of the High-Tech look were derived from the Pop experiments of Archigram (see pp.81–2). High-Tech matured in the design of the iconoclastic Pompidou Centre, by Richard Rogers (see pp.100–1), Renzo Piano, and Peter Rice (1971–7), and, from then on, in the work of the many architects who had worked with these three, including Eva Jiricna (see pp.98–9) and Jan Kaplicky of Future Systems (see pp.104–5). Although these architects were not concerned purely with style, they offered a look that could be asset-stripped and reproduced in lesser and often gimcrack form, in cafés, in bars, and even in domestic interiors.

In fact, High-Tech soon became a cliché and was short-lived: Norman Foster, Richard Rogers, Eva Jiricna, and Future

Systems went on to pursue a line that pushes different forms of building technology and environmental concerns to new limits. Influenced by the work of scientists, of the aerospace industry, the pioneering work of the American inventor Buckminster Fuller, and environmentalists, architects working in this High-Tech manner are optimists who believe in the notion of progress and in the power of new technology and materials to improve the day-to-day quality of human life. They do not think of themselves as isolated from history. Richard Rogers and Norman Foster both see themselves as part of a Modern architectural tradition that dates back to Joseph Paxton and his Crystal Palace of 1851 in London. Their heroes are engineers and scientists; when Norman Foster was asked to make a film for British television on his favourite building, he chose the Boeing 747 jet.

Left The ultimate in High-Tech: the lunar module descends to the Moon from Apollo 11, in July 1969.

Below Also the ultimate in High-Tech, but of the fictional kind: the interior of the Jupiter mission spaceship, from Stanley Kubrick's 2001: A Space Odyssey, also 1969.

High-Tech styling has softened its focus ever since the bombast of the Pompidou Centre (a "young man's building", says Renzo Piano), yet the spirit of optimism remains ingrained in the world of its leading practitioners. As a street style, High-Tech came and went very quickly in the 1980s. For a brief spell it was a look that went with the wave of matt-black designer goodies that spewed out of the electronic goods industry, and the glum matt-black clothes that young designers and architects felt obliged to wear at the time. If they looked as if they were at a funeral, perhaps they were, although unwittingly: it was the burial of the old forms of industry that had underpinned High-Tech styling, even though very few people would have seen it that way at the height of the High-Tech craze in the mid-1980s.

The High-Tech label, like many stylistic tags, can be misleading. Of all the architects to whom it was lightly attached, Norman Foster might have the most reasonable grounds for resenting being grouped with those for whom contrived visual effects seemed more important than design quality. Foster's technological credentials, like those of Michael Hopkins, have always ensured that a building's appearance, however expressive, has grown out of structural needs rather than the temptation to make an eye-catching gesture.

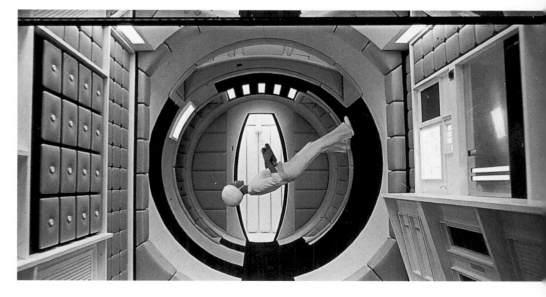

INDUSTRIAL SPACES

PROFILE

PRINCIPAL ARCHITECTS:

Benjamin Thompson, member of T.A.C. (The Architects Collaborative, with Walter Gropius)

Gary Cunningham

PRINCIPAL COMMISSIONS:

Faneuil Hall and Quincy Street Market, Boston, Massachusetts, renovated in the 1970s

South Street Seaport, New York, renovated in the 1980s

Power Station House, Dallas, Texas, renovated in the 1980s

Industrial conversions began as a logical response to a rapidly changing world. As service industries replaced manufacturing ones, vast buildings and industrial complexes lay empty, inviting demolition or adaptive reuse. Benjamin Thompson, a leading exponent of urban renewal, rehabilitated Faneuil Hall and Quincy Street Market in Boston, Massachusetts, in the 1970s. The buildings were reinvented and refurbished as public recreation and retail areas – a revolutionary idea at the time. In London, Covent Garden, a disused fruit and vegetable market, underwent the same transformation in the 1980s, while domestic conversions became commonplace in New York.

The vernacular of industrial conversions was established in exposed stairs, beams, and girders and sandblasted brick. The new aesthetic was refined by the Moderns, as in Gary Cunningham's exemplary Power Station House in Dallas, Texas, now converted to a dwelling. Its new elements complemented the old space, the original internal divisions were respected, and an exposed stair echoed the functional configurations of the past while sporting elegant timber treads.

Gary Cunningham's 1980s renovation of a Dallas, Texas, power station into a private residence exemplifies the successful response to the design challenge of newly abandoned warehouses, market halls, and factories from the 1970s onward. The original structure is maintained but Cunningham has given it an updated Modern design twist.

Left *Eva Jiricna's apartment for Joseph Ettedgui, featuring Eileen Gray's "Black Magic" screen, is part of the seamless body of work she produced for the fashion designer's cafés, shops, and homes.*

Right *Ettedgui's Modern kitchen is a nautical food processing area: everything is stowed away behind polished stainless steel, as in a ship's galley.*

EVA JIRICNA

PROFILE

BORN:
Prague, 1939

EDUCATED:
University of Prague, Prague

PRINCIPAL COMMISSIONS:
Joseph Shop, Mayfair,
  London, 1980
Joseph Ettedgui Apartment,
  Knightsbridge, London, 1985
Legend's Nightclub, Mayfair,
  London, 1986
Joe's Café, South Kensington,
  London, 1986
Joseph Shop, South
  Kensington, London, 1988
Spirit Zone, Millennium
  Experience, Greenwich,
  London, 2000

Eva Jiricna left Prague for London in 1968 shortly before Alexander Dubcek's liberal government was suppressed by Moscow. After working for nine years for the architect Louis de Soissons, she got together with Richard Rogers (see pp.100–1) – working notably on the stylish interiors of the Lloyd's Building – before setting up in practice on her own. In teaming up with the fashion designer Joseph Ettedgui for a number of projects – including the Joseph shops, café, and three homes for Ettedgui himself – Jiricna developed a style that made an essentially systematic and industrial look appear glamorous and welcoming.

In her first interior for Joseph and in her own striking apartment, Jiricna used a palette of highly contrasting materials and colours – black, white, and chrome offset by bright green studded floors, factory reds, and yellows. Over time, this hard vibrancy gave way to a more delicate and more sensual use of materials and colours. It could be said – and very much as a compliment – that Jiricna had become the new Eileen Gray (see pp.28–9). She continued to experiment with powerful engineering forms and structures: the stainless-steel and glass stairs she introduced into a number of interiors are both lithe and beautiful as well as being thorough-going works of lightweight engineering. The genius of her interiors is that, at their best – as, for example, in Joe's Café, in London – they appear almost ethereal, and yet are rational and built to last.

Above *The striking stainless-steel galley kitchen and open-plan living room of John Young's apartment, showcase High-Tech materials and technology. Note the triple-height glazing, polished concrete floor, and circular, wall-mounted radiators. The chairs are by Eileen Gray (1926).*

Right *A lightweight steel stair rises through the three upper storeys of Rogers's house. Architectural intervention has been kept to a minimum to maximize the sense of space. The chairs are by Arne Jacobsen (1955).*

RICHARD ROGERS & JOHN YOUNG

PROFILES

RICHARD ROGERS

BORN:

Florence, Italy, 1933

EDUCATED:

Architectural Association,
London,
Yale University, New Haven,
Connecticut

JOHN YOUNG

BORN:

Chelmsford, Essex, England,
1944

EDUCATED:

Architectural Association,
London

PRINCIPAL COMMISSIONS:

Pompidou Centre, Paris,
 1971–7
INMOS Research Centre,
 Gwent, Wales, 1982
Lloyd's Building, City
 of London, 1979–86
Court of Human Rights,
 Strasbourg, France, 1989–95
Channel 4, London, 1990–4
Judiciary Building, Bordeaux,
 France, 1993–9
Millennium Dome, Greenwich,
 London, 1999

Richard Rogers's career began in the 1960s with Team 4, a partnership that also included Norman Foster (see pp.102–3). The firm had a reputation for designing cleanly packaged industrial buildings enlivened with the odd technological flourish. After Rogers and Foster parted, it was Rogers who championed the dramatic (sometimes even theatrical) approach of exposing and celebrating a building's services and functional mechanisms. In Britain, Joseph Paxton's Crystal Palace of 1851 was a model; the steel-and-glass building was transparent, revealing itself in a way that owed nothing to arbitrary façades or grand historical references. The summation of the Rogers "let it all hang out" approach is represented by the Pompidou Centre in Paris (designed by Rogers with Renzo Piano and Peter Rice) and the Lloyd's Building in London. Rogers's love of displaying the viscera of a building also found its influence in Archigram (see pp.81–3 and 94), the movement led by Peter Cook and Ron Herron and based at London's Architectural Association in the early 1960s. Their gleefully impractical ideas were meant to stimulate, but Rogers was the architect who, more than most, would carry their spirit (and with it the zeitgeist of the period) into the real world.

Rogers's brand of High-Tech lent itself well to interiors where structural demands were less stringent and the celebratory aspect of technological elements could be fully explored. Rogers's own house conversion in Chelsea (the capital of smart hippie London) was an early example. More recently, John Young (an influential partner in Rogers's firm from the Pompidou Centre onwards) designed a dramatic apartment for himself adjacent to the office's headquarters in West London. Both of these typify Rogers's contribution to the Modern visual lexicon: revelation – and celebration – of a building's most functional elements.

NORMAN FOSTER

PROFILE

BORN:

Manchester, England, 1935

EDUCATED:

Manchester University,
Manchester, England,
Yale University, New Haven,
Connecticut

PRINCIPAL COMMISSIONS:

Willis Faber Building, Ipswich,
  England, 1975
Hong Kong and Shanghai
  Bank, Hong Kong, 1979–86
Communications Tower,
  Barcelona, Spain, 1994
American Air Force Museum,
  Duxford, England, 1997
Chep Lap Kok Airport, Hong
  Kong, 1998
Reichstag reconstruction,
  Berlin, 1999

By the late 1990s, Sir Norman Foster had become as much a global brand as an architect. With a staff of over 500 and projects such as the colossal Chep Lap Kok Airport, Foster and Partners was among the world's most successful practices. Commentators described the British practice as the new Skidmore, Owings and Merrill, the vast and hugely efficient New York and Chicago firm, famous for its slick corporate office blocks in its 1950s heyday. The difference between Foster and SOM, however, is that the former remains committed to pushing the limits of architectural design and constantly pursuing new solutions for new opportunities.

Foster's fascination with aerospace technology, lightweight materials, and buildings made to precise tolerances has led to a wave of instantly recognizable structures. Each shimmers with light, is mostly held in check by a taut skin, and lands as gently as an airship. Foster's designs are notably controlled – unlike the exuberant buildings of his one-time partner, Richard Rogers (see pp.100–1). Foster's own home is an expansive penthouse on top of his dramatic office on the Thames at Battersea, London. As with all his projects, the space is arranged to seem almost boundless – a feeling encouraged by the sparse palette of colours (normally confined to silver, gray, and white) and materials. The roof allows the sun to bring in its golds, pinks, and oranges.

The generous interior
landscape of the Foster
penthouse has the feel
of an art gallery, and is
designed to be as
light, uncluttered, and
unrestricting as possible.

FUTURE SYSTEMS

PROFILES

JAN KAPLICKY

BORN:

Prague, 1937

EDUCATED:

College of Applied Arts and Architecture, Prague

AMANDA LEVETE

BORN:

London, 1955

EDUCATED:

Architectural Association, London

PRINCIPAL COMMISSIONS:

Glass House, Islington, London, 1993

Wild at Heart flower shop, Notting Hill, London, 1997

Architects' own house, Notting Hill, London, 1998

Press Pavilion, Lord's Cricket Ground, London, 1999

Ark Pavilion, Earth Centre, Doncaster, Yorkshire, England, 2001

Future Systems is a London-based firm that is much influenced by the technologies from aerospace, boat-building, and other industries that specialize in lightweight materials and equipment, space spin-offs, and aircraft design. Its dream has been to touch the earth as lightly as possible with its gentle, elegant, and sophisticated designs.

Founded in 1979 by Czech-born Jan Kaplicky with David Nixon, the practice took a while to take off as it struggled to win major public commissions, but in the 1990s, with new partner Amanda Levete, these began to come in. What brought the firm into the limelight was some of its less ambitious projects such as the Glass House in north London, commissions initiated by individuals and families who want their homes to resemble space-ships. These homes have an ethereal quality that suggests that everyday life is not a solemn burden. The houses have a holiday feel, and, although distinctive and sometimes quirky in their details and their very bright colours, these are relaxed and gentle homes.

In 1999, Future Systems developed the first large monocoque (a construction in which the outer shell carries all or part of the stresses) building, the egg-like, all-aluminium Press Pavilion at Lord's Cricket Ground in London. Commissioned by London's Marylebone Cricket Club as a highly expressive machine for journalists and broadcasters, it is a monocoque structure composed of seamless welded aluminium panels curving over aluminium ribs, like the construction of a boat or modern aircraft wing. If the right clients can be found, then the monocoque house will soon to be sure to follow.

NEO-BAROQUE

This was a phenomenon rather than a self-conscious type of style, which emerged in London when the Punk movement ran out of steam. It was a loosely connected camaraderie of designers, architects, artists, magazine writers, editors, and young antiques dealers, who were all scraping a living and making homes out of bits scrounged from trash bins, brewed up as a way of looking at design and making architecture that was as wild and original as the Punk explosion had been in 1976–7.

It involved a generation of creative people who had grown up in London and who enjoyed the latest things in fashion, art, music, and design, as well as old furniture, fabrics, and prints – anything, in fact, that could be bought cheaply in markets or salvaged from rubbish dumps.

The upshot was a fusion of the wilfully, and even aggressively, in-your-face new and the most Baroque and unfashionable of the past. Add to this a desire by designer-makers like André Dubreuil (see pp.114–5), Tom Dixon, and Mark Brazier-Jones to realize a fusion of new and old designs in unlikely materials – welded iron and steel – and the result was an explosion of style-mongering that was looked down on by the architectural establishment, but which caught the imagination of a young public.

The architectural input was given mostly by the ebullient Nigel Coates (see pp.110–1), who had been teaching a rather subversive course at London's Architectural Association from the late 1970s. The whole thrust of the Neo-Baroque movement (not that anyone called it this at the time) was one of connecting new ways of living in the city – grandly, with verve and style, yet with very little money – with new movements in art, music, architecture, and design that were primarily London-based (there was no such coherent equivalent in Europe or the United States).

Looking back, the early works of Dixon, Dubreuil, and gang seem crude and a little too deliberately subversive; yet there was something there that was to catch the imagination of a new wave of club and restaurant owners, furniture collectors, young homemakers, and advertising agencies. Dubreuil's series-produced "Spiral" chair, for example, became an advertising industry favourite, while his home and studio in north-west London was much in demand for advertising and editorial photographic shoots. The look came together in Dubreuil's studio, in Coates's apartment in Kensington, London, in the pages of *The World of Interiors*, and through Post-Modern films like Jean-Jacques Beineix's *Diva* (1981) and, later, Jeunet and Caro's *Delicatessen* (1991), in which the worlds of subverted new technology and old gadgetry were fused together in a strangely concocted Baroque.

The look became the height of London chic. There was something rather wonderful in seeing displays of Mark Brazier-Jones's biker Baroque furniture in the windows of the Joseph shop, designed by Eva Jiricna (see pp.98–9), just a few hundred yards from the

ultra-traditional Harrods department store in London. There was a touch of Andy Warhol and the Factory in all of this, and perhaps inevitably, this inspired party of designers soon went their separate ways. Dubreuil returned to his native Dordogne in France to make ambitious one-off pieces of modern Baroque furniture. Dixon smartened up and went on to become Design Director for Habitat's furniture shops. Coates matured into one of Britain's most influential architects and urban theorists and became professor of design at the Royal College of Art in London. The ideas of these Neo-Baroquers were to enter the mainstream of popular design in the 1990s. They connected up, too, with other flamboyant designers such as Ron Arad in London and Philippe Starck in Paris. What they offered was a burst of energy in a design and architecture world that was always in danger of taking itself too seriously and, without the genius of a Mies van der Rohe (see pp.20–1) or a Le Corbusier (see pp.18–9), making more purist forms of Modern architecture dull.

Neo-Baroque was in the end a short-lived and strictly local (meaning London) burst of creative energy that was part of London's 1980s Zeitgeist. Having only the superficial appearance of a movement, it perhaps owed more to the illusion of unity that was conferred by style-conscious magazines and other media commentators than to any intrinsic coherence. Even so, the fact that a transitory aesthetic celebrating distressed textures and rich complexity should have been identified at all is an eloquent commentary on the post-Punk era. After self-consciously ugly nihilism comes … what?

For Neo-Baroque there was no immediately available aesthetic formulated by traditional means – no Robert Venturi (see pp.126–7) or Michael Graves (see pp.124–5) to postulate personal theories that might rally designers and architects to a common flag and a developing cause. Instead there was a fast-food need for something new for the media to celebrate, and something new always needs a label.

Neo-Baroque owed little to the intellectual processes of theoreticians or indeed to the more revered and experienced architects themselves, and a lot to the media's need to make apparent sense out of exuberance, and the increasing fragmentation of architectural and design theories. In the end Neo-Baroque was a fireworks display celebrating neither the end of one thing nor the start of the other, but simply itself. The creators and the critics were largely the same people and, predictably, they tended to like what they saw.

Above Bar life in Barcelona: Javier Mariscal's Torres de Avila bar is a theatrical extravaganza topped with a roof terrace with sun and moon towers.

Below left The subversive interior of Caffé Bongo, Tokyo, by Branson Coates Architecture (1985) is made up of elements veering from the High Renaissance to high camp via Mad Max.

Left *The living room of Coates's own apartment is a play of traditional and modern materials, furniture, and decorative objects.*

Right *From the early Neo-Baroque days, a bat-like arrangement of fabric hangs from the wall of the bedroom.*

NIGEL COATES

PROFILE

BORN:

Malvern, Worcestershire, England, 1949

EDUCATED:

Architectural Association, London

PRINCIPAL COMMISSIONS:

Caffé Bongo, Tokyo, Japan, 1985
Noe building, Tokyo, 1988
Taxim nightclub, Istanbul, 1991
powerhouse::uk exhibition, London, 1998
Geffrye Museum extension, London, 1998
Museum of Popular Music, Sheffield, England
Body Zone, Millennium Dome, Greenwich, London, 2000

Nigel Coates never really expected to build. As a tutor at the Architectural Association, shooting a radical and often provocative line, he assumed his designs would remain on paper. From the mid-1980s, however, his work was taken up in Tokyo and he began a career as an architect, releasing some of the zaniest restaurants and bars yet seen anywhere (see p.109). Widely published, these gave him the reputation of being an *enfant terrible* of a Neo-Baroque style that had its roots in youth culture and was in-your-face, up-your-nose, but not ultimately serious. Behind these bravura displays of raunchy, stylistic showmanship was a serious architect and thinker. Coates's own Kensington flat displayed taste and decorum as much as it did wit and energy.

By the late 1990s, his practice, Branson Coates Architecture, had not only matured, but also won major public projects, including the Museum of Popular Music, and the Geffrye Museum extension, and had shown how these could be provocative, practical, and beautifully made. His architecture has been characterized by the use of unexpected materials, sudden changes in scale, and the flowing patterns of circulation through them. Each building is an adventure.

Left The apotheosis of Punk – the dining room of Marco Pirroni's London apartment is an architectural representation of the wilfully anarchic music of the Punk movement that swept Britain and America in the mid-1970s. It is a deliberately unsettling space.

Right The radiator, dado rail, picture, and the reveal of a door are sited at crazy angles; walls, ceilings, and furniture were painted throughout by Connor and his assistants.

DAVID CONNOR

PROFILE

BORN:
London, 1951

EDUCATED:
Royal College of Art, London

PRINCIPAL COMMISSIONS:
World's End shop, Chelsea,
 London, 1979
Adam Ant House, London,
 1983
Marco Pirroni Apartment,
 London, 1985
Live TV, Canary Wharf,
 London, 1994

At the Royal College of Art, David Connor teamed up with Julian Powell-Tuck and they set up in practice (later with Pierre d'Avoine and then Gunnar Asplund) as court designers of the Punk Movement, spawned in 1976–7 in London with Malcolm McLaren and the Sex Pistols. While Powell-Tuck kept a rational and more conventionally tasteful eye on the practice's fashionable work, Connor brought to it a strong streak of the irrational and the painterly. Floors, walls, and even doors were arranged at crazy angles, modelled partly on the sets of the German Expressionist film *The Cabinet of Dr Caligari* (1919), designed by Hermann Warm. Strange and gratuitous interior props that were neither furniture nor artworks compounded the unsettled look.

The idea was realized at its most extreme in the London apartment Connor designed for the Punk guitarist Marco Pirroni, in which the interior style matched the unsettling and near-violent sensation of Punk itself. Punk was based on a kind of aesthetic anarchy, and so Connor sought to subvert and to deconstruct notions of the comfortable modern interior with a sense of the absurd. A fine draughtsman, Connor sketched out his ideas in the form of large coloured drawings and paintings: the Pirroni apartment looks like one of Connor's raw works come to three-dimensional life. Although Punk was short-lived, Connor later constructed a mature aesthetic based on its ideology.

Left Dubreuil's London living room: his iron and metal furniture jousts with superb French antiques and Art Deco favourites. The leopard-skin effect on the steel side table was created by a blowtorch.

Right The swirling metal lines of his desk and chairs clash delightfully with a grand Baroque cupboard, star wall lights, and the tacky plastic-cased desk-top computer.

ANDRE DUBREUIL

PROFILE

BORN:
Perigord, France, 1951

EDUCATED:
Self-taught as a designer and furniture-maker

PRINCIPAL COMMISSIONS:
One-off pieces of furniture
   from 1985
"Spiral" chair, production,
   1986 (can still be ordered)

André Dubreuil came to Britain in the 1970s to work as an antiques dealer, and then in the decorating business Sander Zarach in London's Fulham Road. He had a great knowledge of historic and contemporary furniture, and when he took up a blowtorch and began to weld his own metal furniture during the mid-1980s, he literally fused a sense of history with a very particular vision of the contemporary. His favourite styles were French Baroque and the best of French Art Deco design, personified for Dubreuil in the sophisticated and beautifully crafted furniture and interiors of Ruhlman.

He set up a studio with Tom Dixon, and for a brief moment Dubreuil, Dixon, and other young designer-makers, often labelled under the Creative Salvage heading in design magazines, appeared to be working in the same direction; but differences soon emerged. While Dixon became more contemporary, Dubreuil created a form of new Baroque and, aside from his elegant and simple "Spiral" chair (much used in advertising and fashion shoots in the late 1980s), took a more decorative route. Using richer materials, he created a unique style and way of working, a kind of anthropomorphic Baroque, where animal and insect forms were welded into one-off reinterpretations of historic designs. His apartment above his studio in London's Kensal Rise was a romantic retreat, an Aladdin's cave: mysterious, enchanting. Dubreuil returned to his family's estate in Perigord, where he orchestrated more virtuoso performances in rare metals and rich materials.

Left *The office of Judith Young-Mallin's residential shrine to the Surrealists, complete with portraits of Lee Miller and Jean Cocteau.*

Right *More portraits in Judith Young-Mallin's apartment: to the left of the Steinway, Samuel Beckett, Giorgio de Chirico, Alice B. Toklas, and Ezra Pound look on.*

SURREALIST INFLUENCES

PROFILE

PRINCIPAL SURREALISTS:

Guillaume Apollinaire

André Breton

Hans Arp

René Magritte

Salvador Dalí

Max Ernst

Joan Miró

Elsa Schiaparelli

James Wines, head of S.I.T.E.,
  New York

Steven Holt

PRINCIPAL SURREALIST-INFLUENCED COMMISSIONS:

James Wine, designs for
  commercial interiors, 1970s

Steven Holt, designer of New
  York apartment for Judith
  Young-Mallin

The Surrealist movement in literature and the visual arts flourished in Europe between the two World Wars. A reaction to Rationalism, it was an intellectual movement preoccupied with locating the bridges between the psyche and "reality". To art it introduced the irrational effect as a serious statement. It was founded by poets (Apollinaire and Breton), but its popular influence was ensured by artists. Arp, Magritte, Dali, Ernst, and Miró influenced designers like Piero Fornasetti (see pp.56–7) and Elsa Schiaparelli (whose designs owed a debt to Dalí). When the movement subsided as an intellectual force, its mannerisms and effects endured for the *frisson* they could stimulate. Subtler versions of the simple optical illusion and surreal art images could always be counted on to engage and unsettle.

In the early 1970s, S.I.T.E., a New York multidisciplinary group, created interiors in which plain white walls featured emerging edges of objects and furniture, hints of a past or future frozen into the walls. In the late 1990s the architect Steven Holt transformed a New York apartment into a Surrealist shrine for a client who as a child had been "fascinated with Dali's limp clocks".

Surrealism's objective was to validate the denial of logic. Unwittingly, it bequeathed to the Modern design lexicon a new range of decorative possibilities.

Left *Elizabeth and Gérard Garouste's living room displays both visual sophistication and* faux *authenticity with a hint of frivolity.*

Right *The spare and the surreal are juxtaposed in their baroque-style dining room, which features a Noguchi light.*

GAROUSTE & BONETTI

PROFILES

**ELIZABETH GAROUSTE
BORN:**
France, 1963

**MATTIA BONETTI
BORN:**
Switzerland, 1957

PRINCIPAL COMMISSIONS:
"Moon" lamp, 1985
"Napoli" lamp, 1987
"Dragon" chair, 1988
Nelson Woo's London and
 Hong Kong homes,
 1988–90

Elizabeth Garouste and Mattia Bonetti enjoy a reputation as the *enfants terribles* of English-style decorative eccentricity and French-style conceptualization. Their approach seems always to be a theatrical re-presentation of familiar objects outrageously recast but elegantly finished in the manner of *objets d'art*. Elizabeth's painter husband Gérard Garouste collaborated with them on their first high-profile venture in the late 1970s, the dazzling decor for the Paris night-club *Le Palace*. A fine-art perspective continues to inform their work, with its surreal juxtapositions and subversive use of primitive materials. A chair might be made of straw bales, a mirror can be set in elaborate rockwork – the materials they employ are frequently pressed into alien service or scale.

When they started designing whole interiors they began to theme their objects and create playful narrative strands for their clients. For Nelson Woo's London residence, they used purple and gold triumphal armchairs, and a carpet inlaid with intricate copper panels. For Woo's Hong Kong residence, their cultural dislocations took on a dizzying new turn – Woo specified a theme of *chinoiserie*, and for this they drew inspiration from the Chinese-flavoured decoration in England's Brighton Pavilion. Their legacy is an acceptance of artifice for its own sake. On the surface their designs appear to honour past achievements and future possibilities, but in reality they celebrate an age of increased visual sophistication in which cultural game-playing is elevated by originality and craftsmanship into another strand of the Modern aesthetic.

POST-MODERN

It is hard to pinpoint with any great accuracy the exact entry of Post-Modernism into design and architectural thinking. As far back as the 1930s, architects were playing know-ing games with antique architectural forms and motifs, incorporating them into their work in the guise of witticisms. In London, the Russian émigré Berthold Lubetkin (1901–90) scandalized humourless fellow Modernists by incorporating a caryatid into the portals of his latest Modern apartment house in

Highgate, London. What was this ancient Greek motif doing in an otherwise Rational concrete structure, they wanted to know. The answer was that it was simply a bit of playfulness or whimsy on the architect's part. Full-blown Post-Modernism, however, proved to be quite a different matter. Where architects born at the beginning of the century, like Lubetkin, stayed true to the tenets of Modernism, those born a quarter of a century and more later began to question the ideals and aesthetics of Modernism with increasing vigour after the Second World War. It was not simply that Modern design – white, cool, abstract, unexpressive, aloof – was considered to be old hat, but rather that some felt that Modernism had nowhere else to go. Not exactly born in the USA, but to a large extent raised there, Modernism was a reductivist movement that did not lend itself to America's constant impulse to reinvent itself, an impulse that every new generation of architects is naturally inclined to share.

This rejection of rational, white, progressive Modernism aside, other developments occurred in the world of art and popular culture that architects such as Robert Venturi (see pp.126–7) believed could be incorporated beneficially into the design of buildings, public and private. As Pop sensibilities worked their way into architecture and modern advertising into the mass consciousness, so Post-Modernists translated these populist ideas into architecture, interior design, furniture, decorative objects, and household gadgets. In what the French philosopher Jean Baudrillard called an "ecstasy of communication", designers took up the Post-Modern cause with great abandon. The cause was colour, decoration, and the marriage of high-brow and popular culture.

In his famous book *Complexity and Contradiction in Architecture* (1966), Venturi announced that he favoured messy vitality over cold formalism. Architecture should be inclusive, drawing in images of the everyday. Turning Mies van der Rohe's (see pp.20–1) well-known dictum "less is more" on its head, Venturi announced "less is a bore". In the right hands, Post-Modern design could be witty, subversive, and playful, as well as intelligent and sophisticated. It was all these things, for example, for a few years at least, in the work of Ettore Sottsass (see pp.128–9), whose Memphis studio was a dominant force in product and interior design in the mid-1980s, and Studio Alchymia, led by the architect Alessandro Mendini, the then-editor of the influential architectural magazine *Domus*, also in Milan. However, in less-able hands, Post-Modernism could be far too over the top for comfort. There was always a balance to be sought between populism and banality, the knowing reference and a descent into trivia.

In the United States, a clear-cut Post-Modern style emerged that turned on the work of Venturi, and notably of Michael Graves (see pp.124–5), who personified the switch from Modernism to Post-Modernism. In an earlier incarnation, Graves designed beautiful white, Modernist villas; yet, even then, these were a self-conscious return to the early white houses of Le Corbusier (see pp.18–9), Mies, and, in California, Richard Neutra (see pp.26–7). It is this self-consciousness that characterizes Post-Modern design; sometimes the "jokes" – a split pediment here, an outsized architrave there – appear to be throwaways, rather than thought through carefully on a drawing board. Much Post-Modern design was accused of being cartoon-like, so perhaps it is no surprise that the champions of the style, Michael Graves among them, began to design for the Disney Corporation from the mid-1980s: the style – populist, colourful, comic – had found a natural home.

Left This kettle with a singing bird was designed by Michael Graves for Alessi in 1985. For the next 12 years, he produced a wide range of domestic ware for this Italian company, beginning with this kettle and ending with a cheese dish topped with a cartoon-like mouse.

Below In this early exhibition set by Studio Alchymia in Milan (1980), familiar Modern designs and household objects are given a wacky new milieu.

The first, zany wave of Post-Modern design had all but petered out by the early 1990s. The way forward for many architects appeared to be a fresh or New Modernism (see pp.136–9), or, like Frank Gehry, Zaha Hadid, Daniel Libeskind, and others, a new approach to Modern architecture – intelligent, sophisticated, and unexpected – that perhaps could only have happened after the grilling Post-Modernism had given to a Modernism that was in danger of becoming tired and emotionless.

Even so, the news of the death of Post-Modernism in architecture may be exaggerated. In many other areas the Post-Modern attitude of being both sincere and ironically allusive at the same time has been so completely absorbed into Western culture that a label is no longer even necessary. Sometimes it seems that the whole of popular culture at the present time is Post-Modern. Middle-aged pop singers like Cher who might once have been relegated to the nostalgia circuit now top the music charts as archly refurbished versions of their youthful selves. Movies quote their own sources and influences incessantly. Novels from the 1990s like Thomas Pynchon's *Mason & Dixon* rejoice in their artificial historical form. A knowing TV series like *The Larry Sanders Show* scurrilously depicts a fictitious US talk show and yet it attracts real celebrities as guests. *The Jerry Springer Show* is a grotesque but self-aware distortion of a once-sincere confessional TV format. A thousand shopping malls in the United States and Europe that never make the design magazines still ransack the Post-Modern bag of tricks as a matter of course. In the real world – the world that Robert Venturi so vehemently championed in *Learning from Las Vegas* (1972) and in which we all live – the legacy of Modernism is considerably harder to identify.

Left *This typically circular internal space by Michael Graves is for his Crown American Realty Trust Headquarters Building (1989). Graves was responsible for both the architecture and all of the interior designs.*

Right *Graves designed this domestic interior for Charles Jencks with playful Classical effects in mind.*

MICHAEL GRAVES

PROFILE

BORN:

Minneapolis, Minnesota, 1934

EDUCATED:

University of Cincinnati,
Cincinnati, Ohio
Harvard University, Cambridge,
Massachusetts
American Academy, Rome

PRINCIPAL COMMISSIONS:

Hanselmann House, Fort
  Wayne, Indiana, 1967
Kalko House, Greenbrook,
  New Jersey, 1978
Public Services Building,
  Portland, Oregon, 1980–2
Public Library, San Capistrano,
  California, 1983
Crown American Realty Trust
  Headquarters, Johnstown,
  Pennsylvania, 1989
Swan and Dolphin Hotels,
  Disneyworld, Paris, 1990

Michael Graves's career reflects the flux and the questioning nature of Post-Modernism. He first became well known as a member of the "New York Five", a group of architects that also included Richard Meier, Charles Gwathmey, Peter Eisenman, and John Hejduk. In the early 1970s, their common link was a reinterpretation of the 1920s "white" style of Le Corbusier (see pp.18–9). Graves abandoned this model after finding new motivation in the visionary work of the French Neo-classicists Etienne-Louis Boullée (1728–99) and Claude-Nicolas Ledoux (1736–1806), whose grand architectural fantasies combined dramatic expression with simple, monumental, abstract forms. Newly inspired, Graves began experimenting with pastel tones, greater abstraction, and a rejection of unmediated borrowings from historical styles.

Graves's early 1980s Public Services Building in Portland, Oregon, exemplifies his response to civic architecture. Once described as "what a well-travelled child might produce if asked to draw what he recalled from Athens or Rome", the building is a near-cube, 12 storeys high, with playfully modulated motifs and architectural features artfully applied. Quasi-*trompe l'oeil* effects and ambiguous finishes gradually show the building to be less and less simple as it reveals itself. Graves dubs himself a "general practitioner" in architecture, but he is also as well known today for his home furnishings and product designs.

Left This art-flavoured dining room was designed by Venturi and Scott Brown to showcase the pictures of a collector.

Right Here, in an earlier design, the partnership created an exuberant Pop interior for a music room.

VENTURI, SCOTT BROWN & ASSOCIATES

PROFILES

ROBERT VENTURI

BORN:
Philadelphia, Pennsylvania, 1925

EDUCATED:
Princeton University, Princeton, New Jersey

DENISE SCOTT BROWN

BORN:
Zambia, 1931

EDUCATED:
Architectural Association, London

PRINCIPAL COMMISSIONS:
Mother's house, Chestnut Hill, Philadelphia, 1962
Peter Brant House, Greenwich, Connecticut, 1971–3
Sainsbury Wing, National Gallery, London, 1991

Robert Venturi, in partnership with his wife, Denise Scott Brown, since 1967, championed the American townscape as a source of vibrant inspiration. His influential 1966 publication, *Complexity and Contradiction in Architecture,* was a perceptive exploration of the ambiguities and tensions inherent in Western architecture. This was followed in 1972 by an even more seminal book, *Learning from Las Vegas*, co-authored by his partner Steven Izenour and Scott Brown.

To Mies van der Rohe's (see pp.20–1) famous dictum "less is more", Venturi responded "less is a bore". Pluralism, ambiguity, and perceptive psychology were Venturi's watchwords, and Mies's reductivist principles were the butt of his jokes. When in 1984 Venturi designed a range of chairs and tables for Knoll, a firm with its design roots in the Bauhaus, he ran the gamut of playful historical references, saying afterwards "Mies did one chair – I did nine".

Venturi's early 1960s buildings – such as the house he designed for his mother – used the Pop culture trick of celebrating the banal with subtly heightened effects. Some later buildings were criticized as being intellectually cramped, but by 1991 the firm of Venturi Scott Brown was sufficiently established to win the competition for the Sainsbury Wing extension to Britain's National Gallery.

Left The living room makes use of bright planes of highly contrasting colour. Note the unusual tiled floor, theatrical bookshelves, and the cartoon perspective of armchairs.

Right The study area with a curiously distorted plan and "drunken" bookshelves veering off at an unlikely angle from the vertical.

ETTORE SOTTSASS

PROFILE

BORN:
Innsbruck, Austria, 1917

EDUCATED:
Milan Polytechnic, Milan, Italy

PRINCIPAL COMMISSIONS:
"Ceramics of Darkness", 1963
"Ceramics to Shiva", 1964
"Valentine" typewriter, 1969
"TC 800" office terminal system, 1974
Paris office of France's Minister of Culture, 1985

Sottsass, always better known as a product designer than an architect, is one of the key proponents of Post-Modern design. His latter-day approach was highly idiosyncratic: he appeared to want to create a world in which that of the cartoon and that of the banality of everyday life fused together in a colourful and distorted alliance. The result has been never less than vivid, often perverse, and occasionally very funny.

Sottsass is an extremely intelligent architect and product designer with a well-developed sense of the absurd. From 1957 he was senior design consultant to Olivetti, working on typewriters, office furniture, and computers, but at the beginning of the 1980s he gathered a group of like-minded and much younger designers around him in Milan, and, under the name Memphis, the team set about subverting commonplace notions of what everyday objects like vases, chairs, lamps, clocks, and computer terminals might look like. The Memphis effect was extraordinary. Within a couple of years, its loud, plasticky aesthetic, influenced by children's toys, 1950s coffee bars, and shockingly bright colours, had travelled as far afield as Tokyo and Los Angeles. As it became a cliché, so Sottsass changed his tack. In his own apartment, the line between normality and distortion, excitement and calm, is followed with a gentle precision. Only here and there does the unruly cartoon element break out, as in his decidedly off-kilter bookshelves.

Displayed on the mezzanine floor of Chassay & Wilson's Gallery House in London is a selection of their "functional artworks". Housed in a lofty mews, these works and the structure have been fully integrated.

CRAFT REDISCOVERED

PROFILE

PRINCIPAL DESIGNERS:

Tchiak Chassay & Peter Wilson

Lori Weitzner

Danny Lane

Roger Oates

Ron Arad

Ove Arup

One of the virtues of late-20th-century interior design was an increased flexibility toward the role of craft objects and fittings. No longer part of doctrinaire views concerning the merits or otherwise of hand-crafted versus machine-age production methods, craft pieces began to assume the role of precious art objects, designed to enhance a wide variety of domestic and commercial interiors.

Tchaik Chassay and Peter Wilson's Gallery House in London typified the trend. Furniture was either custom-designed for the house or chosen for its sculptural qualities. Even the most mundane detail – light switch, umbrella stand – was immaculately finished to promote the idea of the whole house as art piece. Also in London, the American craftsman/artist Danny Lane, was commissioned to create screens, *objets*, and staircases made entirely of glass – crystal art pieces that often have a functional use. New York textile designer Lori Weitzner successfully translated her interest in traditional weaving and dyeing processes into a series of commercially successful designs, as collections for Jack Lenor Larsen (see pp.162–3) and later for her own design company. In Ledbury, England, Roger Oates's woven work has found its way into domestic interiors as well as into retail outlets. In Glasgow, Scotland, Ove Arup's 1980s Princes Square conversion of an open courtyard to covered speciality shopping centre was dressed with many "traditional" local craft metalwork effects. The results were legitimate but the irony was that the traditional craft skills being celebrated had died out locally and had to be imported.

Thus the perception of exactly what a craftsperson was has shifted from a market-unaware individual selling skillfully-made artefacts on a one-off basis, toward anyone who simply had a direct, hands-on relationship with the materials and the end product. In other words, a non-mass-producer.

Left The barrel-vaulted living room of this country house is made of plywood, and overlooks extensive parklands. The house is steel-framed yet infilled with a rich palette of materials, inside and out.

Right The richly coloured and deeply polished dark red stucco hall opens up to the light and spacious principal living room and the spectacular views.

JOHN OUTRAM

PROFILE

BORN:

India, 1934

EDUCATED:

Regent Street Polytechnic, London

Architectural Association, London

PRINCIPAL COMMISSIONS:

Factory Warehouses, Kensal Rise, London, 1983

Country House, Sussex, England, 1986

Pumping Station, London Docklands, 1988

Judge Institute, Cambridge, England, 1993

John Outram was a fighter pilot before coming down to land as an architect. Perhaps, though, he never did quite land. As he came into his own in the 1980s, he developed a complex style of Post-Modernism that was as much pie-in-the sky as common sense. On the one hand, Outram's flamboyant buildings were richly, even wildly, decorated and made use of inventive and colourful materials. On the other, and underneath their amazing, dreamcoat skins, they made efficient use of energy and employed lightweight materials.

The country house Outram designed for a Swedish billionaire as a venison farm was a truly extraordinary mix. A single-storey villa attached to a polychrome Victorian conservatory, it was steel-framed but covered in various forms of polished concrete that looked like sweet licorice and nougat. Inside, the lightweight steel frame allowed Outram to create graceful arched rooms – lined in polished plywood and other light woods – that were bright and gracious. The entrance lobby, though, was a lustrous play on Neo-classical precedent: it was only when visitors passed through the lobby into the main suite of rooms that they entered a realm of sunshine and lightness. This was one of the few new country houses built at the time; most of the rest were designed in various tweedy and clumsy pseudo-Classical styles that were never as convincing as this. In later years, Outram's work became increasingly flamboyant and weighed down with metaphors, narratives, and illusions that only he understood.

Left This full-height living room in the Bjornsen House in Los Angeles is both an art gallery and a means of framing views beyond the house – a complex and essentially Post-Modern device.

Right The staircase in the Museum of Contemporary Art in Los Angeles are almost a return to pure Modernism until you catch a glimpse of Isozaki's Post-Modern furniture.

ARATA ISOZAKI

PROFILE

BORN:

Oita, Kyushu, Japan, 1931

EDUCATED:

University of Tokyo, Tokyo, Japan

PRINCIPAL COMMISSIONS:

Festival Plaza, Expo 70, Tokyo, Japan, 1966–70

Gunna Prefectural Museum of Modern Art, Takasaki, Japan, 1971–4

Kitakyushu City Museum of Art, Kitakyushu, Japan, 1972–4

Fujimi Country Clubhouse, Oita, Japan, 1972–4

Bjornsen House, Los Angeles, California, 1988

Museum of Modern Art, Los Angeles, California, 1996

Isozaki's work is both monumental and highly eclectic. Having studied under Kenzo Tange, who brought the ideas of Le Corbusier (see pp.18–9) to Japan, Isozaki worked with his former professor for 10 years on major building projects that were an important part of the development of the Modern movement outside Europe and America. In 1973, he married the Japanese sculptress Aiko Miyaki, and his work underwent a change. He became fascinated by the possibilities of sculptural form and the work of monumentally sculptural architects from the past such as Etienne-Louis Boullée (1728–99) and Claude-Nicolas Ledoux (1736–1806). This led to the development of a Post-Modern style incorporating heroic Neo-classical and Baroque elements, a highly mannered approach that was a long way from his Corbusian roots through Kenzo Tange.

Throughout the 1970s and 1980s, Isozaki's work became increasingly ambitious: the buildings were extremely clever, but critics thought they lacked soul, and felt that their forms appeared to be gratuitous. That, though, was the spirit of Post-Modernism. By the 1990s, Isozaki appeared to have moved into a more sober and reflective phase, as witnessed in the elemental simplicity of the Bjornsen House and the Museum of Modern Art in Los Angeles.

MINIMAL TO NEW MODERN

Partly as a reaction to what they perceived as the excesses of Post-Modernism in its 1980s heyday, many younger architects returned to the surety of a cool, white Modernism, albeit stripped of its earlier moralizing. This was especially true in Europe, but also in the United States, where Modernism was seen more as a style – the International Style – rather than as a crusade. The upshot was a fresh wave of crisp,

Above *John Pawson's spare and serene white lines are much in evidence in the bathroom of the Saatchi House (1987) in London.*

Below right *The camera-shy Ann Demeulemeester, Antwerp's Minimalist couturier, appropriately lives and works in Belgium's only house by Le Corbusier.*

Previous page (left) *Barbro Bahm's Minimalist Ice Chapel is part of the 1998 version of The Ice Hotel, an annual winter structure built of ice slabs from a frozen lake in Jukkasjärvi, Sweden.*

Previous page (right) *This reductivist table by Maarten van Severen bears all the hallmarks of Minimalist design.*

clean-cut architecture and interiors composed of light, bright, flowing, and, above all, clutter-free spaces. This New Modernism was not a movement, more a common thread running through a wide range of designs. There were obvious points of reference: the mezzanine floor (useful in an age of expensive downtown property), white walls, wooden floors, open stairs, open-plan kitchens (the less they were needed, the bigger these tended to be), and huge, built-in cupboards for storage. Most of these were purely practical concerns. There was little meaning or symbolism in these pared-down designs, but that was partly the point. In an age in which we had become bombarded with imagery and had little time to stop and stare or simply to daydream, the home, above all, needed to be, or could be, a place of quiet refuge. If there were to be meaning, then this could be found in books, music, and conversation. Perhaps it makes sense that this New Modern sensibility emerged at a time when the professional middle classes were working harder and longer hours; more and more people needed peace and calm in their busy lives – the last thing they needed was a fussy home.

Taken to its logical extreme, the home might become almost entirely free of possessions. This was the course adopted by architects and designers who became labelled Minimalists, of which John Pawson (see pp.140–1) and Claudio Silvestrin became Zen masters from the mid-1980s. Pawson and Silvestrin, who were professional partners for some years, developed an architecture in which the walls and surfaces were all-important. Silvestrin, an Italian-born architect based in London, focuses primarily on domestic projects, interiors, small gardens, and retail design. He has also designed what may well be the smallest exhibition space in Europe. The White Cube (1993) is a project room for contemporary art located on the first floor of a building in London's St James's, an area surrounded by Old Master galleries and specialist art bookshops and close to Christie's auction rooms and the Royal Academy. The space is indeed literally a white cube – in design terms – the end of the line when it comes to neutral exhibition spaces.

Hotels and fashion stores are other establishments that needed to decide which side of the line they were on: rich and luxurious or plain and simple. The Hempel Hotel in London ("conceived" by Anouska Hempel) is not alone in taking the Minimalist route. In the fashion world, John Pawson's 1995 interior for Calvin Klein's boutique in the old Neo-classical Manhattan Life Building on Madison Avenue in New York ran against the opulent trend of the time. Meanwhile, Peter Marino specialized in creating airy stripped-down spaces for both Valentino and Donna Karan. In such projects the crossover between product (superior

accommodation or fashion items) and premises is simply an inevitable consequence: in leisure and fashion a coherent image is everything.

Some of the hallmarks of a home by Pawson and Silvestrin included serene white spaces washed gently with diffused light in which one walked barefoot. Bathrooms that were simply a wooden tub, adopted from Japan, and a stone basin set on stone floors. Kitchens that seemed little more than a solid work counter and a range of cupboards. Doors that reached from floor to ceiling so as not to interrupt the passage of monastic white walls. Furniture built into the fabric of the house. These were part of an aesthetic that became increasingly popular among the ever-growing wave of single people working hard in cities, and for those who came to see the home not as a "machine for living in"

as Le Corbusier (see pp.18–9) said, and certainly not as a messy family maelstrom, but as a quiet retreat from an ever-tougher and more competitive world outside.

You could argue that the obvious impracticality of such Minimalist domestic interiors made them more akin to personalized exhibition spaces than places for real people with real possessions and real habits to live in. That, though, would not necessarily be a criticism: if the client's lifestyle required such a space then Minimalist designs fulfilled the brief, pure and simple. The style worked best for those sufficiently financially comfortable to afford a second home, usually in the country, where they could store all those

Above Anouska Hempel's design concept for the 1990s Hempel Hotel in London may look simple and monastic but the materials used are not. She is adept at capturing the mood of the time, as in Blakes, her 1980s period-style London hotel.

things they meant to throw away when they adopted Minimalism, but did not have the heart to do so. Ironically, the spare, bleached designs of Pawson, Silvestrin, and other Minimalists might be seen to owe as much to the underlying thinking of the early Post-Modernists (see pp.120–3) as to the Modernists who preceded them. If Modernism were at heart an inflexible creed, then Post-Modernism was a much more liberal invitation to pick and choose from the historical dressing-up box something that matched the mood and the times. Those hard-working achievers who sought refuge in Pawson and Silvestrin's uncluttered domestic interiors would not remain upwardly mobile or single forever, and so theirs was more probably a lifestyle choice made to match the passing moment than a commitment to any strongly felt aesthetic.

Left The architect Claudio Silvestrin built this holiday home in Majorca for a German client. It is the essence of Minimalism, or as Gertrude Stein said about San Francisco, "There is no there there."

Above The living room and kitchen of Pawson's west London house have been converted from the shell of a conventional Victorian house. The original cramped interior has been opened up radically to create a light-filled space.

Right The bathroom in Pawson's house has a wooden tub that is made of simple materials. It is designed to be drenched in steam and water while retaining its Zen-like sense of calm.

JOHN PAWSON

PROFILE

BORN:

Halifax, England, 1949

EDUCATED:

Architectural Association,
London

PRINCIPAL COMMISSIONS:

Waddington Galleries, London,
1983

Saatchi House, London,
1987

Wagamama restaurant,
London, 1992

Calvin Klein store,
New York, 1995

Architect's own house,
London, 1995

John Pawson came relatively late to architecture after travelling and living in Japan in the 1970s. The traditional Japanese house and the culture that is a part of its design and way of life inspired him to think of ways in which the same spirit could be transferred to Modern houses in the West. The result is his refined, elemental approach to architecture and interior design (although, with Pawson, the two are one and the same thing).

His approach has been described as Minimal, yet there is a richness in the work that challenges this label. His interiors are never simply conventional rooms stripped to their basic and painted white, but rather holistic and timeless architectural ideas made real. Floors are lovingly crafted from the best wood; doors and doorways are exceptionally generous, often reaching from floor to ceiling. Fixtures and fittings are solid and intended to be permanent – marble basins, oak tables, slate worktops. Walls and ceilings are white, yet, as Pawson points out, there is white and white. He uses warm white paints a world apart from the harsh chemical whites used by many architects. These walls often conceal deep, full-length cupboards in which the clutter of everyday life is hidden. Walls are bare. Pawson loves art, yet he abhors paintings on walls. Free from visual distraction and mess, the Modern Western home can achieve a Zen-like spirit of tranquillity and repose. In practice, his approach to architecture is an expensive one. It requires high standards of craftsmanship and the best materials. It might look easy to create such architectural purity, yet, as his imitators have found, it is a way of designing that requires foresight and an all-encompassing vision of not just how a house might look, but how it will feel and be lived in over a long period.

Left *The living room in Lee House, Tokyo, faces the dining room across the courtyard garden. The deep lacquer of the traditional furniture offsets the polished concrete block walls.*

Right *The Lee House is built on half levels connecting the garden courts of different character. These are linked by ramps, an idea developed by Ando's hero, Le Corbusier (after whom he named his dog), in the Villa Savoie (1928–31), at Poissy-sur-Seine, France.*

TADAO ANDO

PROFILE

BORN:

Osaka, Japan, 1941

EDUCATED:

Trained as a boxer and later as a builder; self-taught as an architect

PRINCIPAL COMMISSIONS:

Koshino House, Ashiya, Hyogo, Japan, 1981

Church on the Water, Tomamu, Hokkaido, Japan, 1988

Church of the Light, Ibaraki, Osaka, Japan, 1989

Lee House, Funabasi, Tokyo, Japan, 1991–3

Temple on the Water, Awaji Island, Hyogo, Japan, 1992

The Japanese architect Tadao Ando designs houses and places of worship of profound concentration and almost ineffable beauty. His trademark is unadorned poured concrete walls, with coarse seams and studded with holes at regular intervals. Such spaces are unusual, and sometimes seemingly over-scaled, and yet they form a wonderful blank canvas for the light patterns that are made by the sun as it enters the rooms throughout the day.

In the Koshino House, concrete is used as magnificently as stone, the narrow slits and broad shafts of daylight playing across the walls with the certainty of a great abstract painter at the height of his powers. Here there is little or no need for decoration, much less for pictures or wallpaper: the play of light on Ando's great walls is enough. The Koshino House is an example of how Ando creates serenity and an austere religious beauty from the Modern house. This is a place for ritual and quietude, a still place in a world that seems, to human beings at least, to be not so much turning as spinning like a top. This is a very particular aesthetic and one that many people brought up in a world of pattern, decoration, colour, and objects would find difficult to adjust to. But, the more our societies become lightning-paced and our nerve-ends frayed, the more appealing Ando's reductivist vision becomes.

Left *The interior of the Villa Dall'Ava is a complex meeting of intersecting walls and spaces and a rich play of contrasting materials.*

Right *The rooftop swimming pool shows how the Villa Dall'Ava is raised in different sections among a gridlock of 19th-century houses. The house is on an axis with the Eiffel Tower.*

REM KOOLHAAS

PROFILE

BORN:

Rotterdam, Holland, 1944

EDUCATED:

Architectural Association, London

PRINCIPAL COMMISSIONS:

National Dance Theatre, The Hague, 1980–7

Villa Dall'Ava, St Cloud, Paris, 1991

Lille Station Shopping Complex, Lille, France, 1991–5

Kunsthaal II, Rotterdam, Holland, 1992

"The more architecture mutates," says Rem Koolhaas – architect, teacher, former journalist, and cultural subversive – "the more it confronts its immutable core." Koolhaas was the leading light of OMA – Office of Metropolitan Architecture – which started life as a body of like-minded architects in the mid-1970s and whose supporters were beginning to rethink the role of architecture in terms of its relationship with the city. Since then, OMA has developed into a full-blown architectural practice based in Rotterdam, although it retains its distinctive quizzical approach to the design of buildings.

The questions Koolhaas began to ask were based around a quest to integrate architecture more fully into the city life, to have buildings become a part of the narrative, spoken and unspoken, of the great metropolises. One way of doing this was to deconstruct buildings and architectural styles and to reform them in ways that questioned the architect's role as form-giver while, inevitably, creating new forms. These new forms, as the Villa Dall'Ava in Paris shows, were provocative assemblies of different Modern styles, unexpected meetings, and even clashes, of materials, and the bringing together of numerous design strategies. The idea is to reflect, and celebrate, the richness and complexity of the contemporary city. Yet, as Koolhaas admits, this search for a new, critical Modern architecture – "another" architecture – is difficult not least because "architecture is like a lead ball chained to a prisoner's leg: to escape he has to get rid of its weight, but all he can do is scrape slivers off with a teaspoon".

Left Andrée Putman's schemes fuse the overtly classic with pared-down chic. This hotel bedroom, encased in mahogany, typifies her style: sleek, elegant and lacking in frivolity.

ANDREE PUTMAN

PROFILE

BORN:

Paris, 1925

EDUCATED:

Paris *Conservatoire*; worked as a journalist for *L'Oeil*

PRINCIPAL COMMISSIONS:

Interiors for:

Morgan's Hotel, New York, 1984

Karl Largerfeld store, Paris, 1984

The Orchid Club House, Kobe, Japan, 1985

Office of Jack Lang, Minster for Culture, Paris, 1985

Hotel Wasserturm, Cologne, Germany, 1989

Sets (in collaboration with Peter Greenaway) for *The Pillow Book,* 1996

Designs for furniture (new and reproduction), lighting china, interiors, and scenographs

Andrée Putman has built an international reputation as an interior designer as a result of some highly publishable projects that identified her as an eclectic and sophisticated stylist with a keen sense of history. In the 1960s, after studying music and working as a journalist, a meeting with Denise Fayolle led to her creating designs for the French chain store *Prisunic*. This diverse start set the tone for a career devoted to the idea of beautiful things for everyone.

Her charisma is part of her influence upon Modern design: she operates as a self-styled prism through which a single cultural style is fused together from theatre, objects, décor, fashion, film, painting, and architecture. Her furniture creations – whether utilitarian or art pieces – suggest a blend of modernity that is both classic and chic. Her influence upon Modern design is her cultured perspective: a style born of individual taste and judgment rather than manifesto.

In 1978 she established her firm, *Ecart*, where she and her design staff produced textiles, lights, china, interiors, and furniture reproductions by designers such as Eileen Gray (see pp.28–9) and Mariano Fortuny. Thereafter, her most influential work has included Morgan's Hotel in New York, The Orchid Club House in Kobe, Japan, and stores for designers such as Yves Saint Laurent, Karl Lagerfeld, and Azzedine Alaia. With Wilbert van Dorp she created sets for Peter Greenaway's *The Pillow Book* (1996), a style-saturated movie featuring interiors with rich vernacular detailing in a scheme of theatrical intricacy and elaborate lighting. Described as "illusory authenticity", it recalls similar effects in her hotels, where "authentic illusion" might equally apply. Her design firm also produces interior projects, scenographs, and furniture for the middle market.

SETH STEIN

PROFILE

BORN:
London, 1959

EDUCATED:
Architectural Association,
  London
Royal College of Art, London

PRINCIPAL COMMISSIONS:
Own house, Knightsbridge,
  London, 1995
Mews House, Knightsbridge,
  London, 1997
Mandelson House, Notting Hill,
  London, 1998

Seth Stein worked for both Norman Foster (see pp.102–3) and Richard Rogers (see pp.100–1) before setting up in practice on his own. He represents, in many ways, a generation of architects and designers for whom the old, preacherly, and moralistic teachings and direction of Modern Movement thinking were all but irrelevant. For Stein and his contemporaries, Modernism is a way of experiencing the world and designing for it free from dogma. The houses he has designed are thus relaxed and colourful, despite being rational, geometrically grounded, and making use of new technology and materials when they seem appropriate.

His own house is based around a courtyard and mixes the latest sculptural furniture by Marc Newson with old Andalucian waterpots and colours based on those of Luis Barragán (see pp.160–1). A cultural tourist in the best sense, Stein has also made knowing references to the work of, among other Modern architects he clearly admires, Tadao Ando (see pp.142–3) and Le Corbusier (see pp.18–9). Although easy-going and free from gratuitous technologia, Stein's work can incorporate mechanical novelty when the aesthetic effect is worth it. The car lift that brings its owners' canary-yellow Fiat 500 as a kind of artwork into the living room of the Kensington, London, mews house he built for a client, is a delightful and nicely detailed intrusion. It makes playful use of limited space and brings a neat twist of drama into this otherwise cool and collected home. Stein's studied yet apparently relaxed approach to domestic design dovetailed neatly with the ethos of "easy, modern living" that was promoted by *Elle Decoration* magazine, and its copyists, in the mid-1990s.

The Mediterranean and perhaps even California come to London via Stein's relaxed Modern styling in his own home, in which his courtyard squeezes every last bit of daylight out of the short English summer.

Left Designed by Wolf, this stark interior features a painted concrete floor and white plaster walls, into which he has added an antique chair, velvet squab cushion, and gilt bench covered in white cotton.

Right To achieve this reserved look, Wolf has used neutral colours – beige, dark brown, and white. The couch was adapted from a metal-framed bed, and has softening pillows.

VICENTE WOLF

PROFILE

BORN:

Cuba, 1945

EDUCATED:

No formal training in interior design

PRINCIPAL COMMISSIONS:

Interiors for:

Prince and Princess Von
  Furstenberg

Clive Davis, President, Arista
  Records

Rick Goldstein, Design
  Director, Gap Stores

LS Collections retail stores

Products:

Neidermaier furniture

Schumacher carpets

Sirmos lighting

Wolf was raised in Cuba, and relocated to Miami in 1961 during the Cuban Revolution. A lack of education seems to have driven him to succeed. Learning by looking, he frequented museums and design homes, absorbing different influences. Meanwhile, he took various jobs in the media: fashion, modelling, acting, and advertising, the common link being that he was fired from all of them.

He finally landed a job at the Decoration & Design Building in New York, sweeping floors and folding samples in the stockroom, and eventually selling fabrics and design interiors with a partner, Bob Patino. In 1988 he started his own business with no office, no assets, and no clients. When the jobs began coming in, Wolf's lack of any formal schooling suddenly became a strength. Like Andrée Putman (see pp.146–7), he brought a highly personal set of visual references to the design process. Influenced only by how he feels about what he sees, Wolf has arrived at an aesthetic that is spare, restrained, and controlled.

Wolf claims to build his interior effects on three levels. First comes the architectural part in which the backgrounds are established. Into this setting go the sculptural elements – the furniture for that particular space. Finally there is the painterly aspect in which the colours are created and balanced to complete the room. Eclectic contents and a claim that money has nothing to do with style typify a credo of New Modernism, and Wolf's as well, with the designer seen as a cultural filter for multifarious elements disposed in a restrained setting.

Left Much less is more: in this Van Duysen-designed kitchen, all of the necessities have been included but they have been stripped down to their bare essentials.

Right A sleeky stuffed ottoman and couch are the only nods to "comfort" in the severely restrained design of this living room.

VINCENT VAN DUYSEN

PROFILE

BORN:

Lokeren, Belgium 1962

EDUCATED:

Higher Institute of Architecture, Ghent, Belgium

PRINCIPAL COMMISSIONS:

Chloe shop, Zele, Belgium, 1985

Anvers showroom, Antwerp, Belgium, 1993

De Backer-Van Duysen residence, Gent, Belgium, 1994

System shop, Antwerp, Belgium, 1999

Selfridges shop, London, 1999

The interiors of Vincent Van Duysen reflect a precise and considered aesthetic that is really the taste of the designer himself, repeatedly reinterpreted in response to location and mood. During the mid-1980s, Van Duysen, a trained architect, flirted with *avant-garde* design in Milan, working for Sottsass Associati (see pp.128–9). He had some brief design collaborations back in Belgium, and then established his own architect's office as well as his own distinctive approach to minimalism.

Van Duysen is reluctant to identify influences and movements as they can devalue the distinctiveness of his work. "Minimalism? I prefer to speak of essentiality," he says. Certainly many of his domestic interiors have a spare look that is offset by the tactile qualities of fine wood and linen, and a few voluptuous cushions. Colour and textural combinations and exotic references are finely judged. In his rarefied world a sense of the orient is evoked by introducing a few dark wood elements; Mediterranean kitchens are suggested solely by masonry elements, and Japanese-style apartments take their effects from size, scale, and colour. When he converted an old Belgian house, he treated it both as a sanctuary for the busy owners and a reflection of their personalities. A fireplace holds its original position even after an extension was built around it – part of his conservation process. To Minimalism he has brought a modern approach in which decoration is inherent in colour and texture, and the ultimate goal is always the comfort that comes from the peacefulness of controlled space and a restrained palette.

Left *Lee Mindel's apartment in Manhattan is both dramatic and refined, with attention to detail being paramount.*

Right *Contemporary classics by Mindel's favourites feature heavily in the apartment. In this room, the Ox chairs are by Hans Wegner.*

LEE MINDEL

BIOGRAPHY

BORN:
New York, 1953

EDUCATED:
University of Pennsylvania;
and Harvard

PRINCIPAL COMMISSIONS:
Ralph Lauren headquarters,
New York, 1991

Lee Mindel's great skill has been to seamlessly mix the arts of architecture and interior decoration. The upshot has been a run of houses, apartments, and offices in New York and Long Island of great sophistication. Furniture, fabrics, and artworks are never added as an afterthought, but as part of a Modern flow: everything goes together and appears to do so easily. In his earlier designs, notably in his own apartment near Washington Square, Mindel created a Modern architectural frame that could house an eclectic meeting of furniture and *objets* from across the centuries and around the world. This approach gave new life to antiques that could have been crusty and a little too "art historical" elsewhere, and made historical artefacts a part of the Modern world.

Never afraid of colour and rich, warm surfaces and materials, Mindel moved to a rigorously white, Modern format with the design of his beautiful new apartment. He used a limited yet subtle palette of creams, grays and whites, creating warm tones from colours that in many other architects' hands would be hard and edgy. Mindel's knowledge of all periods of furniture enabled him to balance designs defined by a strict, rectilinear geometry with more flowing and even organic pieces. It is the balance of these, the gentle play of daylight, the craftsmanship of the wooden floors, and the detailing that make this the sort of Modern city apartment that even the most strict traditionalist might secretly covet.

GLOBAL

The rise of the Modern Movement was inseparable from that of Cubism, the stylistic revolution in painting created by Georges Braque and Pablo Picasso from around 1905. What is intriguing is that Braque and Picasso's sensibilities had taken a new path after the 1900 Paris Exhibition, where artists were confronted by people, artworks, and objects across the French Empire, with strong representations from North and sub-Sarahan Africa

Right The bedroom of the La Gelta apartment in Paris by Marie-France de Saint-Felix, is a womb-like hideaway leading off an underground swimming pool and connected to it by a small, vaulted saloon. The walls are made of river sand, lime, white cement, and powdered ochre from the Roussillon mountains.

Below right This rough-hewn chaise longue designed by Jérôme Abel Seguin was inspired by Balinese craftsmen. It was carved with traditional tools using wood that Seguin purchased locally in Bali.

Previous page (left) Using the principals of Feng Shui, Seth Stein carefully positioned this mirror to encourage the flow of energy through this house.

Previous page (right) This heavily textured, rope-covered, hand-finished piece was made by the Kenja Samburu tribe. Its ethnic design has influenced some jewellery styles in the West.

and from the South Pacific. The artists incorporated African themes into their work. In a sense, then, the Modern Movement, which was always universal in spirit, rose with a form of Globalism in art. The world may have shrunk, but the outlook of artists and architects had grown immeasurably. However, most Modern architects before the Second World War, and many for a long time after that, saw artworks from Africa and elsewhere as exotic and "primitive" and employed them to offset the machine-age aesthetic of their own making, or simply as lovely objects in their own right. What has happened since is that not only has mass travel allowed people from all over the world to visit and get to know other parts of the world, but there has been a mass migration of peoples from the former colonies of the French, Belgian, German, and British empires to Europe as there has been a mass of refugees – Jews, Poles, Russians, and Central Americans – to the United States. This has had a domino effect in architecture and design: the artistic cultures of Africa and the South Pacific are no longer seen as "primitive" in developed countries, but as offering a complementary aesthetic and set of meanings to their own countries and to the West as well, while Chinese and Indian philosophies are similarly embraced: think of the popularity of Feng Shui.

Even so, distant cultures are still seen as being exotic in the sense of glamour and sensual appeal; we are attracted by the shapes and colours rather than the culture that produced them. Nevertheless, our increasingly Global take on the world has allowed us to make our homes more romantic and colourful than ever before. From the fabrics of Jack Lenor Larsen (see pp.162–3) to *Colors* magazine produced for Benetton, we have come to appreciate Global design. The interesting thing in the 1990s is the way in which this design has been internalized by designers, architects, and decorators and the extent to which it has been applied. In the works of furniture designers in the late 1980s, such as Garouste and Bonetti (see pp.118–9) in Paris and Sue Golden in London, the influence of tribal sources was clear, yet reinterpreted – wildly by the former, calmly by the latter. What we have seen since is a two-way process whereby European, American, and other designers, like Jérôme Abel Seguin (see pp.166–7) have gone to live and work in the countries that once came as a novelty to the great exhibitions (Paris 1889, Chicago 1893, Paris again in 1900) in the industrial world, while an increasing number of designers

Above This colourful sari fabric is from India. Its delicate pattern has translated well to Western tastes and traditions.

from the cultures once considered "primitive" are now working in Paris, London, and New York. The result is new fusions of art, design, music, fashion, food, and architecture. Architecture, which both reflects and shapes society, does so at a slower rate than the ever-accelerating arts and media. Just as its responses must move at the pace of building processes, its subsequent influences may also be slow to arrive. Often this process has had unexpected effects: The Eiffel Tower, the Sydney Opera House, and the Empire State Building are now better-loved than when they first appeared. Moreover, the architect as self-appointed social worker is nothing new: Norman Foster once responded to an invitation to build a marina on one of the Canary Islands with an all-embracing plan to revitalize the island's social structure and even improve its climate by moving forests. Another example is the new cultural centre Renzo Piano designed for New Caledonia in the South Pacific. A building for the islands' Kanak Indians, this is a subtle and spectacular meeting between the sensitivities of one of Europe's most inventive architects and a culture with which most of us are unfamiliar.

Global design is at its best when it fuses different traditions and cultures, as if seamlessly. The best example of this fusion was the work of Luis Barragán (see pp.160–1), the Mexican architect who brought the colour and religious energy of his native country into a Modern architecture that fitted Mexico like a glove. Here was none of the mismatch of design and local culture that has ruined towns and cities in developing countries over the past 50 years. Whenever two cultures respect one another, the result for design and architecture can only be beneficial: one usually gains the technology it lacks, the other the spirit it has lost while developing that technology.

Left For his quill designs, Christian Astuguevielle has drawn inspiration from primitive cultures. The grand architecture of his Paris apartment provides a superb counterpoint to his creations and a fitting setting to rope furniture and African sculptures.

Barragán was an unrivalled
colourist, as the Gilardi House
in Mexico City demonstrates.
One of his later works (1976),
it is almost abstract
expressionist in character.
The inspiration for its vibrant
colours is Jesus Reyes
Ferreira's painting Fighting
Cocks. Although the house
is a very solid structure,
the interior does have
ethereal moments.

LUIS BARRAGAN

PROFILE

BORN:
Guadalajara, Mexico, 1902
(d.1987)

EDUCATED:
Escuela Libre de Ingenieros,
Mexico City; self-taught as
an architect

PRINCIPAL COMMISSIONS:
Ildefonso Franco House,
  Guadalajara, Mexico, 1929
Mago Vazquez House,
  Chapala, Jalisco, Mexico,
  1940
Prieto Lopez House, Mexico
  City, 1948
Galvez House, Mexico City,
  1955–6
San Cristobal Stud Farm,
  Mexico City, 1968
Capuchinas Chapel, Colonia
  Tlalpan, Mexico City, 1955
Gilardi House, Colonia
  Tacubaya, Mexico City, 1976

Luis Barragán had a truly wonderful eye for colour. He brought deeply and richly saturated colours to his buildings in Mexico, proving that Modernism need not be clinical or monochrome. More importantly, the colours he used were often rooted in natural pigments rather than the chemical-based paints that many Modern architects tended to use. This makes his buildings much more a natural part of the landscape than those of his contemporaries. He coloured his sensual yet rigorously proportioned and fundamentally simple buildings with the eye and palette of a painter. The results are often achingly beautiful. Perhaps it is because Barragán approached architecture from a sure mixture of rationalism and romance that he felt little or no need to follow in the long shadows of the Bauhaus (see pp.16–7), of Mies van der Rohe (see pp.20–1), and of other influential movements and great architects, whose work was perhaps purer in a puritanical sense, yet in many ways less engaging than his own.

Oblivious to the burgeoning Modern Movement in Europe and the United States, Barragán began building in styles that were influenced by Moroccan and Islamic architecture, decoration, and colour. He was taken by the pools, gardens, and terraces of the Alhambra in Granada, Spain, and their inspiration never left him. The San Cristobal Stud Farm is clearly influenced by such architecture, yet at the same time it owes as much to Mexican architecture and its unsurpassed sense

Left Once owned by Jack Lenor Larsen, Judy Bergsma's home reflects Larsen's fascination with natural architecture and materials. The influences are the Bantu tribe's building methods, and the bird sculpture is from the West African Senufo tribe.

Right Luxurious quality as a buffer against mass production: a Larsen interior expressing his philosophy of natural effects and high-quality finishes.

JACK LENOR LARSEN

PROFILE

BORN:

Seattle, Washington, 1927

EDUCATED:

University of Washington, Seattle, Washington
Cranbrook Academy of Art, Bloomfield Hills, Michigan

PRINCIPAL COMMISSIONS:

Draperies, Lever House, 1952
Wall-hangings Exhibition, Museum of Modern Art, New York, 1968
Silk hangings for Sears Bank and Trust Company, Chicago, Illinois, 1978
Dinnerware collection for Dansk International Designs, 1980
Upholstery collection for Cassina, Italy, 1980

Larsen is an idealist who sits on the horns of a dilemma that all the great idealistic craftworkers and designers have sat on: he makes beautifully designed and highly crafted fabrics and wall-hangings that adorn many great works of architecture, but these, by their very nature, are too costly for those for whom he would like to design. Larsen's principal concern, other than that of his own art, is that everyone in an age of alienation and speed deserves a home that is like a sanctuary, a place of beauty and repose away from the neurotic bustle of the city. His own home is just that – a gentle showcase of natural materials and design ideas culled from many countries.

Although he made his name with draperies for the Lever Building in New York (designed by Skidmore, Owings & Merrill; this innovative office block launched thousands like it from its 1952 completion), he has travelled the world as well as his native American west coast in search of inspiration. His favourite fabric designs, he has said, are from pre-Columbian Peru and Sassanian Persia, and also from Japan, China, and Brazil. He is a great admirer of the works of Mariano Fortuny, Louis Tiffany, and William Morris. He has an inquisitive and appreciative eye that allows him to be that rare thing: a Modern designer with a Global perspective across both space and time.

Left *Sergio Puente and Ada Dewes's Jungle House is an adobe hideaway in San Bernabe, a suburb of Mexico City. It was constructed by local builders using indigenous materials.*

Right *There are no solid walls in the Jungle House, which they describe as being "open air", resulting in the interior space merging seamlessly with the jungly ravine outside.*

SERGIO PUENTE

PROFILE

BORN:

Mexico City, 1952

PRINCIPAL COMMISSIONS:

Jungle House, Mexico City,
  Mexico, 1985
Architect's own house,
  San Bernabe, Mexico,
  1989

There are architects whose philosophies emerge from their built achievement, and others who build little or nothing and instead are theorizers of what buildings could be like. Sergio Puente and Ada Dewes are closer to the latter, although they have created buildings that dramatically express their preoccupation with the ultimate kind of organic habitat: buildings literally absorbed into the landscape.

Puente is an architect and planner concerned with the nature of the city, in particular with the apocalyptic environmental disaster that his native Mexico City has become. With Dewes he has created houses that stand in almost totemic denial of traditional dwelling technologies. Their Jungle House in a village southwest of Mexico City combines conventional amenities like running water, electricity, and drainage with a steeply raked staircase symbolic of an Aztec pyramid, and a palette of ethnic building materials – the adobe bricks came from a demolished house in the locality. (Ironically Puente had to teach the locals traditional adobe building methods, including how to add river-washed pebbles to the joins between the blocks.) The platform that acts as a roof to the sleeping quarters is also the topmost floor, its roof and ceiling provided by lush surrounding foliage. Puente's jungle structures are fuller versions of the louvered barriers found in traditional houses in Singapore and Malaysia – graduated interfaces between inside and outside. They offer yet another model to Modern designers, one of cavities and layers enmeshed in the landscape, not placed statically on top of it.

Left *At his island house in Bali, Jérôme Abel Seguin's "wooden wall" separates the main room and the verandah.*

Right *The interior of Seguin's dining room features some of his huge stock of 20-year-old teak that he uses to make his furniture.*

JEROME ABEL SEGUIN

PROFILE

BORN:
Bordeaux, France, 1950

EDUCATED:
Ecole Boulle, Paris
Ecole des Beaux Arts,
Paris

PRINCIPAL COMMISSIONS:
Furniture and sculpture for
  Hermes, Air France, Louis
  Vuitton, Club Mediterrannée,
  Aman resorts, Meridien
Island Woods Exhibition,
  Galerie d'Art Archide, Paris,
  1994

After a successful career as a sculptor in Paris and Sao Paolo, Brazil, Seguin went to Bali in the mid-1980s, fell in love with it as Gaugin had Tahiti a century earlier, and decided to stay. He made several visits to the islands of Indonesia before settling on Sumbawa, where he built his house and workshop. In the 1990s, other European artists and designers followed in his "escapist" footsteps, in order to design natural homes, Modern in spirit, a long way from the cultural and physical climate of "hothouse" London, Paris, or Berlin.

What drew him to Indonesia, apart from the climate and natural beauty, was the remarkable choice of unfamiliar materials with which he could work. He originally sculpted in glass, mirror-glass, and plaster; now he works in pieces of old wood – santigi, jackwood, teak, and kalengo – that he buys from Javanese merchants, island boatmen, and fishermen. Whatever wood he finds, he transforms into original pieces of furniture carved with traditional tools and hand polished. Among these are beds, chaise longues, benches, tables, consoles, and screens. Seguin also makes abstract sculptural works based on the natural forms he sees while walking through the forest, or else based on vernacular architecture. He has become a kind of Robinson Crusoe of the design world, creating Modern yet natural forms from the things he sees and the materials he comes across day-to-day in his "desert island" retreat.

DIRECTORY

ARCHITECTS/DESIGNERS

Tadao Ando Architect & Associates
5-23 Toyosaki 2
Chrome
Kita-ku
Osaka
Japan
Tel: 81 6 375 1148

Ron Arad
62 Chalk Farm Road
London NW1 8AN
England
Tel: 0171 284 4963

Staffan Berglund Arkitektontor AB
David Bagares gata 5
111 38 Stockholm
Sweden
Tel: 46 8 612 2339

Branson Coates Architecture
23 Old Street
London EC1V 9HL
England
Tel: 0171 490 0343

Mark Brazier-Jones
Hyde Hall Barn
Sandon
Hertfordshire SG9 ORU
England
Tel: 01763 273599

Chassay & Last Architects
Berkeley Works
Berkeley Grove
London NW1 8XY
England
Tel: 0171 483 7700

Nigel Coates
see Branson Coates Architecture

David Connor International
10 Ivebury Court
325 Latimer Road
London W10 6RA
England
Tel: 0181 964 5357

Gary Cunningham Architects
4136 Commerce Street
Suite 200
Dallas
TX 75201
USA
Tel: 214 821 9525

André Dubreuil
Paris
France
Tel: 01 42 27 85 02

Foster & Partners
Riverside Three
22 Hester Road
London SW11 4AN
England
Tel: 0171 738 0455

Future Systems
See Jan Kaplicky

Garouste & Bonetti
Paris
France
Tel: 33 14 35 75 007

Gallerie Yves Gastou
12 rue Bonaparte
75006 Paris
France
Tel: 01 53 73 0010

Frank O. Gehry Associates
1520B Cloverfield Blvd
Santa Monica
CA 90404
USA
Tel: 310 828 6088

Michael Graves Architect
341 Nassau Street
Princeton
NJ 08540
USA
Tel: 609 924 6409

Steven Holt
435 Hudson Street
New York
NY 10014
USA
Tel: 212 989 0918

Michael Hopkins & Partners
27 Broadley Terrace
London NW1 6LG
England
Tel: 0171 724 1751

Arata Isozaki & Associates
6-14 Askasaka 9
Chrome
Minato-ku
Tokyo
Japan
Tel: 3 405 1526-9

Charles Jencks Architect
19 Lansdowne Walk
Holland Park
London W11 3AH
England
Tel: 0171 727 8216

Eva Jiricna
7 Dering Street
London W1R 9AB
England
Tel: 0171 629 7077

Philip Johnson
885 3rd Avenue
Apartment 2540
New York
NY 10022
USA
Tel: 212 319 5880

Jan Kaplicky
21c Conduit Place
London WC2 1HS
England
Tel: 0171 723 4141

Pierre Koenig
California
USA
Tel: 310 826 1414

Rem Koolhaas
Rotterdam
Holland
Tel: 31 10412 3349

Danny Lane
19 Hythe Road
London NW10 6RT
England
Tel: 0181 968 3399

Jack Lenor Larsen
New York
USA
Tel: 212 462 1300

Imre Makovecz
MMA
Kecske Utca 25
H-1034
Budapest
Hungary
Tel: 00.361.388.1701

Javier Mariscal
Estudio Mariscal
Pellaires, 30-38
8819 Barcelona
Spain
Tel: 34 3 303 3420

Lee Mindel
see Shelton, Mindel & Associates

John Outram
16 Devonshire Place
Hampstead
London WN1 1PB
England
Tel: 0171 262 4862

Andrée Putman
83 avenue Denfert-Rochereau
75014 Paris
France
Tel: 01 55 42 88 55

John Pawson
Unit B
70-78 York Way
London N1 9AG
England
Tel: 0171 837 4949

Sergio Puente
Calle del Carmen 34
Calonia San Bernabe
Octopec Magdelona Contreras
10300 Mexico DF
Mexico
Tel: 52 554 101 16

Richard Rogers & Partners
Rianville Road
Thames Wharf
London W6 9HA
England
Tel: 0171 385 1235

Marie-France de Saint Felix
52 bichat
75010 Paris
France
Tel: 331 42 39 55 60

Harry Seidler & Associates
Level 5
2 Glen Street
Milsons Point
New South Wales 2061
Australia
Tel: 612 9922 1388

Jérôme Abel Seguin
36 rue Etienne Marcel
75002 Paris
France
Tel: 33 01 42 21 37 70

Shelton Mindel Associates
143 West 20th Street
New York
NY 10011
USA
Tel: 212 243 3939

Claudio Silvestrin
392 St John Street
London EC1V 4NN
England
Tel: 0171 323 6564

Agence Philippe Starck
27, rue Pierre Poli
92130 Issy-les-Moulineauz
France
Tel: 01 41 08 82 82

Seth Stein Architect
52 Kelso Place
London W8 5QQ
England
Tel: 0171 376 0005

Ushida Findlay
41 North Road
London N7 9DP
England
Tel: 0171 700 7754

Vincent Van Duysen Architects BVBA
Lombardenvest 34
2000 Antwerp
Belgium
Tel: 32 3 205 9190

Venturi, Scott Brown & Associates
4236 Main Street
Philadelphia
Pennsylvania 19127-1603
USA
Tel: 215 487 0400

David Whitcomb
404 White Birch Road
Germantown
New York 12526
USA
Tel: 518 828 2846

Peter Wilson
Studio 3
5 Thurloe Square
London SW7 2TA
England
Tel: 0171 589 7560

Vicente Wolf Associates Inc.
333 West 39th Street
10th Floor
New York
NY 10018
USA
Tel: 212 465 0590

John Young
see Richard Rogers Partnership Ltd

PLACES OF INTEREST

Cranbrook Academy of Art Museum
1221 N.Woodward Avenue
PO Box 801
Bloomfield Hills
MI 48303-0801
USA
Tel: 248 645 3300

Design Museum
Butlers Wharf
Shad Thames
London
SE1 2YD
England
Tel: 0171 403 6933

**Eames House and Studio
(Charles and Ray Eames)**
203 Chautauqua Boulevard
Pacific Palisades
California 90272
USA
Tel: 310 396 5991

**Falling Water
(Frank Lloyd Wright)**
PO Box R Mill Run
Pennsylvania 15464
USA
Tel: 724 329 8501

**The Gamble House
(Greene & Greene)**
4 Westmoreland Place
Pasadena
California
USA
Tel: 626 793 3334

Guggenheim Museum
1071 Fifth Avenue
New York
NY 10128
USA
Tel: 212 423 3500

Hempel Hotel
31-35 Craven Hill Gardens
London W2 3EA
England
Tel: 0171 298 9000

**Hill House
(Charles Rennie Mackintosh)**
Upper Calhoun Street
Helensburgh G84 9AJ
Scotland
Tel: 01436 673900

**Hotel Parco dei Principi
(Gio Ponti)**
Via Rota 1
Sorrento
Italy
Tel: 081 878 2101

**Horta's House
(Musée Horta)**
25 rue Americaine
St Gilles
B-1050 Brussels
Belgium
Tel: 322 5430490

**Hvitträsk
(Eliel Saarinen)**
SF-02440 Boback
Uusimaa
Finland
Tel: 3589 657 689

**The Ice Hotel
(Yngve Bergquist)**
Jukkasjarvi
Sweden
Tel: 46 980 66800

Museum of Modern Art
11 West 53 Street
New York
NY 10019
USA
Tel: 212 708 9400

The Noguchi Foundation
32-37 Vernon Boulevard
Long Island City
NY 11106
USA
Tel: 718 204 7088

Rose Seidler's House
71 Clissold Road
Wahroonga
New South Wales 2076
Australia
Tel: 612 9989 8020

**Villa Savoye
(Le Corbusier)**
82 rue de Villiers
78300 Poissy
France
Tel: 01 39 65 01 06

Vitra Design Museum
Charles-Eames-Strasse 7
D-79576 Weil am Rhein
Germany
Tel: 4621 702 3200

STOCKISTS

Alessi
143 Fulham Road
London
SW3 6SD
England
Tel: 0171 584 9808
*Product design by Philippe Starck, Michael Graves
and Ettore Sottsass*

The Conran Shop
Michelin House
81 Fulham Road
London SW3 6RD
England
Tel: 0171 589 740

Ecart SA
111 rue St. Antoine
F-75004
Paris
France
Tel: 33 42 78 88 35
Product designs by Andrée Putman and Eileen Gray

Fritz Hansen
20-22 Rosebury Avenue
London EC1R 4SX
England
Tel: 0171 837 2030
*Designs by Arne Jacobsen, Vico Magistretti,
Hans Wegner and Verner Panton*

Habitat
196 Tottenham Court Road
London
W1P 9LD
England
Tel: 0845 6010740 (customer services)

Knoll International Ltd
1 East Market
Lindsey Street
Smithfield
London EC1A 9PQ
England
Tel: 0171 236 6655
and
105 Wooster Street
New York
NY 10012
USA
Tel: 212 343 4000
*Designs by Mies van der Rohe, Marcel Breuer,
Eero Saarinen and Ettore Sottsass*

Thonet GmbH
PO Box 1520
3558 Frankenberg
Germany
Tel: 64 51 50 80
Designs by Alvar Aalto and Marcel Breuer

Herman Miller, Inc
855 East Main Avenue
PO Box 302
Zeeland
MI 49464-0302
USA
Tel: 616 654 3000
Designs by George Nelson and Verner Panton

Memphis
20010 Pregnana Milanese
via Olivetti 9
1–20010 Pregnana Milanese
Milan
Italy
Tel: 392 932 90663
Stockists of Sottsass designs

Vitra AG
13 Grosvenor Street
London W1X 9FB
England
Tel: 0171 408 1122
Verner Panton chair

Viaduct Furniture Ltd
1–10 Summer's Street
London
EC1R 5BD
England
Tel: 0171 278 8456
Maarten Van Severen table

Woka Lamps Vienna
Palais Breuner Singerstrasse, 16
A-1010 Vienna 1
Austria
Tel: 431 513 2912
Josef Hoffmann lamps

Zanotta SpA
via Vittorio Veneto 57
Nova Milanese 20054
Milan
Italy
Tel: 0362 451 038
Designs by Achille Castiglioni

INDEX

ACKNOWLEDGMENTS

The author and publisher would like to thank Graham Vickers for his contribution to the book. Thank you also to all the team at Mitchell Beazley; and to Arlene Sobel, Nadine Bazar, Nicola Kearton, Michelle Pickering, and Ann Parry; and to the homeowners whose interiors are featured in this book.